# Pirate Red Beard Biography. The Complete Autobiography

Mohamed Cherif

Published by Mohamed Cherif, 2024.

PIRATE RED BEARD BIOGRAPHY. THE COMPLETE AUTOBIOGRAPHY

**First edition. May 14, 2024.**



ISBN: 979-8224204618

Written by Mohamed Cherif.

# Also by Mohamed Cherif

**Captain Barbarossa From A Pirate To An Admiral**
Captain Barbarossa: How I Became A Pirate?
Captain Barbarossa: Arruj Death
Captain Barbarossa : I Became An Admiral Over Ottoman
Empire Fleet

**Septembet 11th 2001 Attacks**
UA Flight 93.It Wasn't A Crash

**Standalone**
Mayas & Aliens
The Nazi UFOs Where Are They Now?
Islam As You Never Knew
Scientific Miracles Of Islam In Quran & Sunnah
La Vérité Sur Les Extraterrestres
Blue Beam Project A Zionists-Illuminatis Advanced Weapon
In the 21st Century
Truth About Extraterrestrials

Aliens & UFOs Then & Now
Pirate Red Beard Biography. The Complete Autobiography

# Summary

# Introduction

This is the complete life story of Pirate Barbarossa or Khaireddine Barbarous, who dictated it to his colleague and friend in the sea life the poet and writer Syed Ali Almuradi. He recorded his autobiography after a request of Sultan Soleiman Alkanuni, known as Suleiman the Magnificent.

The individual is the son of his surrounding. What means this proverb? That means his environmental factors and circumstances influence directly and indirectly his thoughts and behaviors along with his life. The fifteenth and sixteenth centuries extended the culture of Piracy, which had been developed worldwide centuries earlier in the Indian ocean, the Atlantic, and the Mediterranean. Piracy was considered as the standard, the norm, and the normal of that age. It was a source of enrichment for ordinary people and for countries. It was practiced by countries implicitly, so many pirates worked for the service of empires. Barbarossa and his brother Arruj were not the exceptions. They were raised in this realm and atmosphere. It wasn't immoral to exercise piracy. Something is clear is that they engaged in piracy after they were regular traders with their ships and after the incarceration and the torture of Arruj the Barbarossa's oldest brother by the Rhodes Knights on his way to Tripoli in Lebanon.

Barbarossa, an Italian term meaning the Red Beard. Mostly the Venetians in the fifteenth century who called Khaireddine Basha or Kheder with this name. Barbarossa or Khaireddine was born on Midilli island (Lesbos today) in 1478. He died in Istanbul in 1546. At a fresh age, he uses the ship as we operate in our days, the cars and all the transportations means. With time, the sea became truly his proper home. A natural person can work outside throughout the day and return at the end of the day to his home to take a rest. Barbarossa took this rest in his ship's private cabinet in the sea's large everywhere.

Through this autobiography, Barbarossa talked about all the events that he lives, saw, or testified about by himself. The spiritual background was dominant in his stories as the antagonists of the Ottoman empire in an aside; the Venice, the Spanish and the Portuguese empires on another side each side represents a theology and his followers the Ottoman empire represents Islam, the Spaniards, the Portuguese and the Venetians represents the Christianity. Using words like Kaffer or kuffar, which means unbelievers or infidels, was frequent.

Despite his strong heart as an adventurer in true life not like in Hollywood movies, I discovered he possesses a highly sensitive soul when the matter concerns his brother Arruj, his siblings, his men, and the poor that he tried consistently to help them everywhere.

Barbarossa never spoke about his mom, his teaching, and his childhood. For example, he didn't reveal that his mommy was a priest's widow before she married his father. He didn't mention that besides the military employment of his father; he was working on pottery and when they started in trading he and his brother Arruj; they sold the pottery of their father outside the Midilli island. Their brother, Isaaq, preferred administrative job, he didn't specify it too.

Barbarossa and his brother Arruj rescued the lives of tens of thousands of Muslims and Jews escaping from the tyranny and the torture of The Spanish Church and transferring them to North Africa and Greece in Salonica.

This autobiography reflects all the cultures, values, morals, and behaviors of all people surviving at that time.

# Chapter 1: The Sultan Decree

I started recording my autobiography after a request of Sultan Suleiman Alkanuni (The Magnificent). In communication with him, it came to me a Farman (irrevocable Sultan decree) from The Sultan Suleiman Khan Ibn Salim Khan this is its text: "*How did you leave you and your brother Arruj Midilli island (Lesbos today) and you opened Algiers? (Capital of Algeria today) What are the 'Ghazawats' (Conquests) that you made on land and sea until today? Write all these events without swelling or reduction in a book and when you finish send me a copy to place it in my library*". When I received this order. I appealed to my comrade, who was beside me in so many conquests on shore and offshore 'Almuradi'. I notified him about the Sultanate's Farman, thus we started, I dictate and Almuradi writes.

# Chapter 2: Native Roots

When Mohamed ElFateh opened Midilli island in 1462, he directed the Turkish communities to settle there. My dad was one of the initial immigrants and a descendant of one of the Knights of Sibahia (the Sultan special Knights unit). He too was Sibahian. He gets a 'feudal land' in the area of Wardar (Vardar today) beside the Silanik (Thessaloniki or Salonica today: Greek City) provided for him under an order by the Sultan Mohamed ElFateh when he settled on the island.

So when my father's concerns were rearranged again, he married a young woman from the island's native citizens. My dad was handsome and courageous, my mom gave birth to him four brothers: Isaaq, who was my oldest brother, then my brother Arruj, then me, Kheder, then Elias. May Allah (God) grant all the long age and the Triumph. My Brother Isaaq lived in Midilli Castle meanwhile me and my brother Arruj were fascinated by the sea riding so Arruj bought a ship and worked on her in commerce and for me, I got too a boat with eighteen seats. We were at first moving between Silanik and Agribuse (Euboea or Evia today a Greek island) buying the merchandises and selling them on Midilli but my brother Arruj wasn't satisfied with these nearby distance travels he aimed to sail to Sham's Tripoli (in North Lebanon today). One day, he took my young brother Elias with him direction to Tripoli.

# Chapter 3: Piracy As It Was

My brother Arruj couldn't reach the Tripoli Of Sham as the Rhodes Knights (Crusades defeated in Sham and took Rhodes by force centuries ago) stopped him and he entered a battle with them. My little brother Elias was killed and fell into a martyr. They grabbed all the ships and took them with Arruj to Rhodes, captive and chained. When the information arrived in Midilli, I became profoundly sad, cried a lot, but directly I started seeking for a solution for my brother.

I had a kaffer (Infidel) friend called: Grego a merchant with Rhodes island, I bring him in my ship to Bodrum (Turkish City, the same name until now) and I told him: *"today appears the honest friendship, take these 18000 Akja (Turkish coin) and help me to rescue my brother. Go to Rhodes and watch what's going on there and I'll wait for you in Bodrum."* Grego: *"At your disposal and service."* He told this then he went to Rhodes where he met my brother Arruj Raiss (a name used for the professional sea travelers in the Ottoman empire) and told him: *"Your brother Kheder greets you and he asks Allah to save you, he cried day and night, he sent me to you, he's now in Bodrum and he waits hearing the positive news about you."*

When Arruj heard this, he cried with happiness and he said: *"Greet my brother Kheder, no one should notice the real objective for your coming to the island and we will meet together at the first coming opportunity.*" There was a man called Santerlo Oglo. He came from time to time seeing my brother asking about his needs. One day my brother Arruj told him: "*The Rhodes Knights will never accept selling me to my brother Kheder but I think they'll do with you if you help me to escape from the island I guarantee for you that I'll refund your capital in the future.*" Santerlo Oglo: "*Gladly, if they'll sell you I'll take you, but if I request this directly from them they'll doubt on me, the better is when you visit the town try to walk in front of my market but be prudent to not look at me directly because they'll suspect that we know each other. I'll pretend to see you by coincidence and I hope that the Knights will accept to sell you to me.*" When he heard these words, my brother Arruj became extremely content like he became truly free, how it was so painful for him the captivity life!

After a while, Santerlo Oglo and some Rhodes Knights were assembled in front of his market talking together. He saw Arruj walking in the round trip as he's seeking to serve. He asked the surrounding sailors: "*For whom belongs this prisoner whose leaves and came? He seems strong and effective. I see him always pass here, serving with vitality*! If *his owner agrees to sell him, I'll buy*". One of the Captains said: "*I'm his proprietor. If you want, I'll sell him to you*". Santerlo Oglo: "*How much do you want?*" The Captain: "*I want 1000 dinars* (coin used)". Santerlo Oglo: "*This is an enormous sum!*" The Captain: "*Ok I deliver him to you with just 800*"! Before the sold being completed, the deal was broken, as the Rhodes Knights knew in the meantime, that I sent Grego to buy him. He told them that I'm ready to buy him with 10000 dinars, how a prisoner with a value of

10000 can be sold with just 800, they knew his real value, they retook Aruj and return the 800 dinars to Santerlo Oglo.

After this incident the Rhodesians put Arruj in an underground prison, a dungeon, as a further obstacle to prohibit his rescue and started torturing him oftener than the first time, they placed the chains in his hands, feet and his neck and they give him the enough food just to stay alive not more.

He didn't support all this; he requested to meet the dungeon officer, who asked him: "*What do you want*? Arruj:" *You, what do you want exactly by causing me all this harm?*" The Dungeon officer: *I'm awake about you Turk, you try to save yourself with 800 dinars, your brother Khaireddine Raiss waits for your redemption with the money of the world. Do you think we don't know this or do you expect we are stupid?*" Arruj:" *What's the money amount that should I offer to emancipate me*"? The dungeon officer:" *And you, how much can you pay? How do you rate yourself?*" Arruj: "*I value myself with all the crop of Rumelia* (the South East of Europe which was administered by the Ottoman Empire including: Greece, Serbia, Bosnia, Bulgaria, Croatia, Ukraine, Albania, Slovakia) *from cereals, all the daily expenses paid in AlAnadhool* (south Turkey land) *beside one hundred thousand dinars I offer them for you*". The dungeon Officer: "*Ok, crazy Turk, remain with your mockery. You'll discover how will be your end*". After this dialog, the furious officer ordered the soldiers to persecute him further.

This gets worse results on Arruj, who became desperate and in one night praying and crying, he asked Allah (God) to help him for his love for prophet Muhammud SWS (peace & blessings be upon him) until he slept. He saw an old man with a shiny face telling him: "*Arruj, don't worry about what occurred to you and what kuffar* (Agnostics) *did for you for Islam. Your exit is near"*. He woke up comforted and delighted with this sighting. At that morning, the Rhodesian Captains met together and discussing, one of them suggested: *"days on the sea are changing, today Arruj in jail tomorrow it can be one of us! I think it's not from the intelligence to continue torturing this Turk"*. They put him out of the dungeon and left him as a ship rower. Despite this, Arruj was happy and thankful he said: *" The work on the sea surface is a grace for whom experiencing living in a dungeon. Oh Allah, thank you as I see the world's face"*.

# Chapter 4: Evasion From Rhodes Knights

At this stage, The prince Korkut was governor of Antalya (Turkish City with same name until now). Every year he has a habitude to buy 100 Turkish prisoners and liberate them for the sake of Allah. In this year he sent his Chamberlain to take the hostages. The compromise was to bring them with a Rhodesian ship to the Antalya coasts.

By Allah's appreciation, the chosen ship to transport the detainees was the ship carrying Arruj, but as Arruj was precious to them, he will not be one of the hundred. Arruj was a communicative person. He talks remarkably well with strangers. He has the ability to open new relationships with others. Furthermore, he speaks in various languages like the Romanian as a native born. So many times he enters extended discussions with Rhodesian Captains who coming to his ship. One time, they told him: *"Turkish man, you're a talented speaker, especially with our language. What do you find in Islam? Come and enter our religion, you'll have a tremendous place between us"*. He retorted: *"Oh foolish people, everyone is glad about his religion, does exists any prophet better than the prophet Mohamed SAS (peace & blessings be upon him) to believe in him"*? The Captains: *"So you remain as you're and we will see how your prophet will save you from us and now continue to rowing".*

# Chapter 5: Be Attentive To My Brother

The priest of the Ship talking to the Captains warning them from Arruj: "*be aware of what Arruj saying, don't talk too much with him, he looks well educated he knows about Islam more than I know about Christianity, be careful he's Infidel and Atheist he can mislead you*". The Rhodesian ship docked in an isolated area far away from Antalya, where descended prince's Chamberlain 'Korkut' with the 100 prisoners. They left them there. That night, a strong wind hit the coast. The Rhodesians decided to stay until the morning, then they descended a small boat aiming for fishing. Meanwhile, during the fishing, a harsh storm appeared and prevents the boat from returning again to the ship.

They were obliged to anchoring the boat away from the coast. My brother Arruj took advantage from this opportunity that anyone can't see his neighbor cause of deep darkness, he opened his hands and feet restraints and jump into the water saying: "Bismillah Arrahman Arrahim" (In The Name Of Allah The Mercy and Merciful), he swims and making 'Tassbih' saying 'Subhana Allah' until he touched the land, he makes 'Sujud' (Part of Muslims Prayer) and thank Allah for saving him. Then he walked to a Turkish village. When he turns around trying to know where is he exactly, he finds in front of him a Turkish grandmother telling him: "*it seems that you're arriving from afar travel my son come to my home as a guest tonight*".

She took him to her house she gave him food and clothes. He stayed in this village a complete ten days. Every day and night, they accepted him as a guest. Every night, the inhabitants disputed between them to take him as a guest. For the Rhodesians who discovered the escape of Arruj, they asked each other how do we come back to Rhodes without Arruj? They returned to Rhodes the shame on their faces.

The priest told them that Arruj used sorcery that's why he succeeded in escape. Arruj left the village and oriented his direction to Midilli. He reached Antalya in three days. He found a well-known man called: 'Ali Rais' who owns a ship from the model 'Kaliun' trading on her between Alexandria (Egypt) and Antalya. Arruj was already becoming famous at that stage. He knew him and told him: "*you're welcome my son. This ship is not only for me, it's yours too*". In a matter of a short time, Arruj was the second captain of this vessel.

In the meantime, desperate from the waiting in Bodrum, I returned to Midilli, where I received a letter from my brother Arruj explaining for me his entire adventure. It finally relaxed me to hear good news from him personally.

# Chapter 6: Loss Of The Sultan Ships

The Egyptian Sultan heard about my brother's fame. He invited him to his castle. He asked him to enter his service as he wanted to send a fleet of ships to Indian coasts. If Arruj accepts, he will designate him as an official captain of the Sultanate's fleet. A Royal decree was sent to the governor of Adana (same name until today in Turkey) ordering him to send to Payas harbor (same name until today in Turkey) in Iskenderun gulf (called too Alexandretta gulf) the necessary wood and tools to build 40 Ships. The governor executed the order. Arruj, by himself, got the wood to Payas and had the intention to sail to Egypt. The Rhodesians were informed about all that. They waited for the opportunity to kill Arruj. On his sea road to Payas, they attacked him with a great fleet. Arruj Raiss felt the danger as he conducted the captains to retire the fleet to the coast. He gathered all the sailors to the deep of the Ottoman lands. Then he sent everyone to their native villages and cities. Meanwhile, he returned to Antalya, where he ordered to build a ship with 18 paddles. Later, he attacked Rhodes coasts without mercy and without leaving to anyone of them any breath.

After this attack, the Grand master of Rhodes Knights declared: *"it's appeared a pirate called Arruj, has a ship with 18 seats none can survive from his attacks, he held our money and burn our lands and several times, he kidnaps our men, took them to Sham's Tripoli and sold them in its markets. We arrive in a situation that we cannot yet sailing fearing his atrocities. I warned you and I told you to leave him in the underground prison don't let him out! You didn't listen to me and you made him a rower on the ship. What are you waiting for? Go kill him now!"*

Under this order, the Rhodesians took five or six sea pieces and started searching for Arruj everywhere.Finally, they discovered his ship anchored in a harbor; they burned her, but Arruj and his crew could survive without being hurt and came back to Antalya. His vessel was taken to Rhodes harbor and gibbeted in presence of the Rhodesians, but their failure to capture Arruj made the Grand Master furious. He revealed to them: *"yes this ship for Arruj, but he's not in her"*!

In the hour when Arruj returned to Antalya, prince 'Korkut', the son of 'Biazid Althani' left her and moved to 'Sarokhan' (now Karaman City in Turkey), which will be its new office station as a governor. Prince Korkut has a storekeeper named 'Peyala Bey' who was in the past a friend of Arruj and offered him a 'servant boy'. When he lost his boat, Peyala Bey talked about this to his prince Korkut and described to him how day and night Arruj is fighting against the kuffar and he overcomes them in so many battles. As Arruj's name became well known, he agreed to help him. He invited him and told him joking: *"don't be mournful about your loss, I'll never leave you without a ship"*.

Then he addressed a Kitab (order letter) to Kadhi (Judge) of Izmir (Turkish City same name until now) instructing him: *"When this Kitab reach you, call for the construction of a vessel from the design 'Kalitet' with 24 seats for my son Arruj, he will need it for jihad against the kuffar*". Peyala Bey wrote too a Kitab to the customs director in Izmir telling him: "*Arruj is our brother in Donya (life) and Akhera (Afterlife), serve him, order for manufacturing a ship with 22 places and you must handle this built by yourself. You must deliver it to Arruj on the nearest date and write all the expenses, including all the supplies, in the account of my prince Korkut*". The construction of the two ships took three months and a half. When he reached Izmir, Arruj assembled all his men and sailed to Fujia harbor (Foça today) then to Manisa (Turkish City same name until today) where he resided three days in the castle of Peyala Bey before he met the prince Korkut who praised him so much.

He left them both in Manisa and say goodbye; he paused a night in Fujja praying. In the morning, he led his sea travel with the two vessels. After days he intersected two Venetian ships with model 'Venedic', he ambushed them with 24 thousand dinars on board, the sailors became incredibly prosperous and how they can't be enriched after the Dua (Supplication) of the descendant of Ottomans the prince Korkut for them! Anyone who gains the Dua of the Sultan he will succeed and anybody who is against the Sultan will suffer!

This battle was on Polia coasts (Italian City in Calabria state same name until now). From there he continued to the Rome coasts he met in the sea large of Abiuz island (Ponza island today) other three ships belonging to Venice. When the kuffar see Arruj ships, they started to fire them with cannon shells. As a reaction to this monstrous attack, Arruj started motivating his men and encourages them to counter-attack these ships. The vessels became closer to each other; the sailors jumped on the Venetian ships and occupied all of them. They took 285 prisoners and killed 120 men.

The seized money and merchandises were incredibly huge.When they were transferred to Arruj ships, these last ones were running with the speed of turtles. They bring them to Midilli accompanied by big festivities. Me, my brother Isaaq and our relatives, were awaiting Arruj. We greeted him. Together we hold each other deeply as it was long years we didn't see him since his Midilli's retiring. Arruj decided then to leave Midilli to Izmir to meet his prince Korkut and his brother Peyala Bey. Meanwhile, we knew that Sultan Salim Khan took the Sultanate's throne inheritance from his brother Korkut, who rushes away from worry. Arruj was deceived, my old brother Isaaq advised to him: "*You should quit in the soonest time and spend the cold in Alexandria. Later we will understand what will happen. The ship that you have is from Korkut and this may harm you*".

We didn't have adequate time to fulfill our missing feelings. Arruj left and in a matter of days, he picked up seven ships for the enemy on the coasts of Kerby island (Keros today) and carried them all to Alexandria. At his arrival, the Sultan knew about him coming with 'Yahia Raiss' and seven ships full of booties. Arruj was profoundly embarrassed as he loses all the vessels delivered from Egypt Sultan in Payas, when the Rhodesians raided on them and burned his ship. To win the Sultan amnesty, he offered him some ships from the seven, combining money and spoils. He gifted him too four odalisques and four boys.

The Egyptian Sultan was remarkably happy and satisfied. He honored Arruj and his sailors and he told him: "*Allah is a forgiver. He admires the amnesty, and I forgive you and grant you my reprieve. It's true that you left 16 boats burning, but you didn't let anyone be harmed by fire. You rescued them all and no one was imprisoned. I wasn't offended by the loss of ships. This is typical in life and everything can happen, but I was sad because you didn't come to me directly and inform me by yourself. I heard about the catastrophe from strangers. I excuse you and I thank you because you remembered me and didn't neglect me and ignore me forever."* He expressed all that, and he gave my brother much more gifts than he did.

My brother took permission to quit Cairo and travel to Alexandria. The Sultan issued a conduct to Alexandria's governor to honor Arruj and his companions. As an effect, they spent a wonderful time there. The spring is taking place. My brother, Arruj, wrote to the Sultan for approval to sail. He granted him his acceptance. He rode the sea toward Cyprus coasts where he captured five Venetian ships.

Then he oriented to the west aiming for Djerba island in Tunisia (same name until now) where he marketed his spoils to the sellers. Every sailor took 25 arms from Venice silk, four shooters, four guns, and 171.5 dinars. When he discovered a ship will sail to Alexandria, he forwarded to the Egyptian Sultan a colossal load of Venice silk, shooters, guns, and a boy with 13 to 14 years old. When he received the gifts, the Sultan said: *"if there's an individual in this life who appreciates the grace and the favor to his people, is my son the Captain Arruj"*. The relationship between my brother and the Sultan became deeper and more strong. Then Arruj continued to raid on the enemies' ships. On the coasts of Tunisian Djerba, he seized between five to ten new ships.

# Chapter 7: A Special Love

Came please discovering the country situation, when the Sultan Salim Khan sits on the throne, a conflict occurred between him and his brother Korkut. He sent a complete army looking for him, but they couldn't locate him. At that time, Captain Basha (official status on the sultanate's folk) 'Iskandar Basha' was a terrible autocrat and unfair because he didn't let anybody ride the sea, even in a small boat with two paddles. He often punishes the sailors on the grounds that they're Korkut men.

When I perceived all this, I chose to leave Midilli, I charged my ship with wheat and headed to Sham's Tripoli where I changed wheat with barley, later I moved to Brevez (Greek 'Preveza' City today) where I sold my barley and I purchased some mares and mules. Then I anchored on Aya Mavri island (Greek 'Lefkada' island today).

In the face of Bruza (the name of his ship), I saw a vessel with 24 seats docked in the harbor. I liked her so much. I asked about her owner, they told me that his name is Captain 'Abdel Fattah'. Captain Fattah was newly deceased, his successors sent the ship there to sell it. I fell in love with this ship and I was ready to pay any amount of money to his proprietors. In the end, they agree to sell it with six bags of silver. When I owned this ship, I felt like I own the entire world. I rode my new ship,

I took the other ones and I crossed the Mediterranean East and West, North and South until I reached Djerba island. I met my brother Arruj there.

Meanwhile, We study in our future station, it appears to us that we travel to Tunis (then and now the capital of Tunisia) and we added: "*As the death is the end of every alive, it could be for the sake of Allah*".

We were three: me, my brother Arruj and Yahia Raiss, each one took a ship we arrive in Tunis, we enter to the Sultan, we presented him our gifts and we suggested to him: "*we would appreciate that you allow us a place to secure our ships and be a leading site for jihad in the sake of Allah, we will sell the booties in Tunis markets and the Muslims will benefit from that .The commerce will flourish and we will pay for the state treasury the eighth of spoils.*" The Tunisian Sultan answered: "*What do you claim is certainly rationale, you're welcome, the country is yours.*"

# Chapter 8: A Blessed Sultan

The Tunis Sultan received us. We spent the winter in 'Halk Alwadi' Harbor. When the spring appeared, we cruised the sea with five pieces. My vessel was the quickest one, we enter on Sardinia island (Italian island same name until today) and there we grabbed a pirates' ship carrying 150 prisoners. Meanwhile, we were on this ship, It emerged from a distance an immense ship like the 'Kechiche' mountain Waliadhu Bellah (God forbid). My right arm 'Delly Mehmet' who was a Captain for one of our ships, known for his bravery and courage, revealed to me: *"My Commander, please authorize me to seize this ship"*.

I didn't prefer to contrarian him, I accepted, he accomplished this. His vessel was undoubtedly small in comparison with her. Then we pursued this ship. When we approach it, we discover it's empty. No person is there. When the pirates saw us, they picked up their light boats and riding away. They leave behind, a vast ship full of wheat. We congratulated 'Delly Mehmet' and saying to him: *"Ghazw Mubarak* (blessed Conquest)". In the next morning we captured other two ships. One of the two was charged with honey, cheese and olive. The other one was a Venetian ship loaded with iron. Over weighted with booties, we reached Tunis under the echoes of the cannons. All the men got their parts. We specified the part of the Sultan. We gave so much money for the poor, we earn from them much supplication.

# Chapter 9: A Good Lesson

We spent the cold in Tunis too. When the spring opened its gates; we quit to Naples harbor in 13 days (Italian Port the same name until today). On our way, we came across a full boat sailing to Spain with 300 to 400 warriors. We raised our golden flags, and we started bombarding them. We tried seven times to reach the vessel, in the seventh one we became nearby it, a great battle occurred until we occupied it.

We lost 150 martyrs and 86 were crippled. We realized afterward that it was in all 525 people on the vessel; we detained 183 from them; the rest were already massacred. A governor of a considerable territory in Spain was one of them. After that, we took over another ship. Later, we come back to Tunis where my brother Arruj was treated on his scars in these battles. We got from these battles 70 or 80 parrots and 20 Bazians (bird race) we offered them all to Tunis Sultan.

After these last raids, we became particularly prominent in the enemies territories, simultaneously, they were determined to eliminate us, they asserted: *"it appears two Turks called Arruj and Khaireddine Kheder* (Barbarossa), *we must crush these two snakes before they'll transform to dragons. We should erase their names from the earth's face. If we leave them, they'll cause us too much trouble"*. As a repercussion, they prepared 10 super ships from the design 'Kaderga' to assassinate us, but we were previously in the sea before their arrival. We intended for Genoa, but as the winds were not favorable, we switched to the Alger coasts. We anchored near a castle called 'Bejaya'. The Spanish ships performed the same when they didn't find us in Genoa coasts. We rode the sea at the fastest possible way as the coast clash with them could be extremely risky.

They thought we were avoiding them; they pursued us. After we did a well sufficient distance from the coast, my brother Arruj ordered us to return and get closer to the enemy ships. The Kuffar were confused, as they didn't predict this maneuver. A big battle developed, we conducted a rapid attack on the commanding ship; we captured her with three other ships. The other ones go away to Bejaya, seeking shelter in her castle. My brother Arruj thought of invading the castle and took the six ships. I would prefer to stop him from fearing his health condition. The finest way was to take the four seized ships to Tunis and leave the rest.

# Chapter 10: Ten Ships In My Hands

My brother Arruj didn't listen to me. He issued his orders to attack Bejaya castle, which was teeming with Spanish soldiers. Moreover, their colleagues joined them from ships seeking refuge under the castle walls. My brother Arruj started the attack under a rainfall of shells and bombs. We lost 60 martyrs and a remarkable number of burns. We were about to take over the castle, but my brother Arruj get wounded in his left arm by a shell. When the Spaniards saw this, they opened the gates and attacked us. I was so depressed and furious about my brother's state, who was deeply injured.

As a reaction, I counter-attacked them with 300 to 400 men; we tracked them to the castle doors. In this strike, we killed 300 Spaniards and captivating 150. It wasn't convenient to stay long time in front of the castle. My brother Arruj lost his consciousness because of his unsupported pains. I gathered my fighters and directed them to ride on ships; we left the coast under the continuous Spanish bombing on our heads but acknowledges to Allah, no ship was touched. We could return to Tunis with 14 ships. The surgeons cleaned my brother's wounds, but his pains were growing day after day. They told me that his arm must be cut, if I refuse they'll not be responsible for the results. Tunis people were incredibly content when they saw us returning with 14 ships after we withdrew with just four, but when they noticed Arruj's state, they fell into tears. I announced to the Surgeons: "*Anyone Who can recover the arm of my brother Arruj, I will offer him his weight in gold and I'll give him too ten prisoners he choose them by himself*".

# Chapter 11: Brother Arruj Arm

The Surgeons met together again to review my brother's health situation; they didn't find any solution other than cutting his arm. I was obliged to accept. They cut it and treated the wounds. I was crying heartedly with deep melancholy. He spoke to me: *"why are you crying? This is Allah's decree and destiny. I thank Allah because I lost my Arm in the battle, this grace satisfying me"*. When the spring returned and the souls refreshed, we went out on eight ships to conquest. We reached Al Andalus coasts (Spain) where the Islamic city 'Gharnatah' (Granada today) newly occupied by the hands of the Spaniards.

The Spaniards were very oppressors for Muslims who most of them were impelled to do secretly their prayers in underground secret mosques. The Spaniards destroyed and burned all the Mosques even when they found A Muslim fasting or praying; they torture him with his family then boiled them all. During that, we brought huge numbers of Muslims, rescue them from kuffar and bringing them to Algeria and Tunis. When we were in Almeria coasts (Spanish City with the unchanged name until today in the province of Andalusia), it looks to us seven ships for infidels; we pursued one of them and grabbed her and because of the winds' direction we couldn't reach the other ones.

The ship that we capture was a Dutch ship loaded with Indian merchandise. From there, we were directed to Minorca island (Spanish island with the same name until today) where we entered a small gulf. It was fifty or sixty days the period that we spend away from Tunis; we penetrated deeper into Minorca; we ran into approximately 200 warriors heavily armed sitting on a riverside. They were grilling a sheep, drinking wine and most of them lost their consciousness.We got seventy to eighty from them and seized five to six flocks of sheep.

Their Chief was brought in to me, I asked him about their intentional orientation, he replied: "*Sir, we knew about your anchoring in Minorca, ten Spanish 'Katerga' ships were planning to hit you via the sea, meanwhile we attack you from the beach*". When I heard that, I attached the prisoners and isolate them by pairs in all the ships, then we moved out from Minorca seeking Genoa, we caught four vessels in our way.

As a result of these takeovers, we became often more distinguished in all the kuffar cities in Europe and they see us as a legend. We raided on Corsica island (French island the same name until today). Later, me and my brother, we headed to Midilli island, our homeland in seven sea pieces.

"Love of the homeland coming from the real faith", is a correct Arabic proverb. When we met our families, we felt the refresh of our hearts and souls. All of our relatives and friends came asking about us. We performed a tremendous festival for seven days and seven nights. Along with it, we provided food for the island's poor, we did the children's circumcision and we married the virgins who has not husbands and to bring happiness to their hearts we held big celebrations, we bought them new dresses.

We brought joy to the hearts of widows, impotent and the disabled. The pockets of our sailors became full of gold until the degree that one of them buy merchandise that cost one Akja with five! And they do this to help the remote area merchants earning more as they displace for long distances and consume more expenditures. They win their supplication and this makes them more confident in the future. Midilli inhabitants served us uncommonly well and so much, they were extraordinarily generous. They brought us the food and fruits begging us to accept them.

# Chapter 12: Sea Is Life

We had the intention of passing the cold on the island. In the meantime, we honored our relatives from the booties' money and we specified our big brother Isaaq with money and Venice's gold. He granted us his grateful 'Dua' but when he saw the missed arm of Arruj, he became deeply sad. One time, my brother Arruj thought of marrying and settle in the island but fastly he changed his mind because his love for the sea was more than anything else. In a morning he notified us he saw a good 'Royaa' (dream sent from God) he stated: "*I saw yesterday the good old man with the white beard that he came for me when I was in custody of the Rhodesians in the dungeon. He instructed me: 'Oh Arruj go to the west, Allah prepares for you so much conquests, glory and honor there'.*

The ships were always coming to Midilli as the Captains bought the captives to use them in the rowing. One day I suggested to these Captains: "*I have an exceed of 827 rowers, I sell them for you*". With that method, I marketed the rowers for the Ottoman merchants captains.

Some of them were valued with 500 dinars, others with 300 and some others less than that. I paid the customs fees for the prisoners that I sold and I delivered to harbors directors their rights. Also, I donated for the Islamic endowments. With that plan, I spent half of the gained money. The other half

I share it with my brother Arruj. We would never like to conserve the money. We used its majority in the equipping of our ships with the necessary goods. The rest we distribute it between our sons. Every man took 90 dinars, their headers took 195 dinars each one. The sailors did not waste their money on the food. Every ship has its own kitchen. The meat was presented twice every week but in so many cases they bought food as the ship's food was not suitable for all of them. When the winter settled, I authorized for some sailors to spend the season in their homelands with their families in the nearby places like "AlAnadhool" (AlAnadhul) and "AlRomelli" (Romelia). As for whom lives in far destinations, I instructed them to spend it with us in Midilli.

This winter, I demanded from the ships' factory in Midilli to construct three ships, one of them with 25 paddles and the two others with 24 each. Thus, we had ten ships by the arrival of the spring. Later, we prepared our ships with the appropriate material, I rode one of my new ships and my brother Arruj rode another one New adolescents coming from Ottoman provinces, especially AlAnadhool and AlRomelli, suggested themselves for us to be sailors on our flotilla as our fame reached them. We choose some of them that we considered they are adventurous and effective. We kissed the hands of my big brother Isaaq, salute our relatives and we left the island in a blessed hour.

# Chapter 13: They Need Our Help

On our way, we took 15 or 16 sea pieces, we conserved the useful ones and we do sink the bad boats. Five of the ships were charged with the wheat and two of them with the olive oil, meanwhile another one with the ivory. The rest were loaded with money and different merchandises. The number of prisoners was 479 women and an infinite number of men. After 29 days of leaving Midilli, we entered 'Halk Alwady' harbor in Tunis with a fleet of ships. We find the locals welcoming us with enormous crowds and great happiness waiting to see us. We saluted them by firing in the air cannons' shells.

The local communities were caring for us. They worried we wouldn't come back again, especially the needy ones who were waiting for us patiently. We gave the wheat for free to the poor and who's in lack, then we sold the rest of the spoils. We sent too to Tunis Sultan his part, comprising 5000 shooters, two maids and four boys from Genoa. Their ages were between 15 to 16 years old. All of them were handsome. If we would market them, their value will be enormous. The Tunis Sultan offered us well equipped luxurious horses.

I and my brother Arruj rode our horses and went to the Sultan's castle, who received us with a considerable welcome voice: *"you honored my kingdom. I beg Allah to make your faces full of pure light in this life and hereafter. You're our Masters".*

When we quit, he granted us too two coats of fur, he also was generous with our men. We spend the winter in Tunis. In the spring, we went out with twelve ships in a blessed hour. We raided on a castle in Sicily (Italian island with the same name until today), we imprisoned 300 captives, dispersing them all in our ships to serve as rowers. Also, 'Delly Mehmet Raiss' caught a commercial ship moored near a harbor packed with sugar. We calculated 650 pairs of sugar boxes.

I ordered Mehmet Raiss to take these booties to Tunis. On the next day, we seized other four boats, two of them were charged with broadcloth. Meanwhile, another one was charged with sailing poles leading to France, the fourth one was with ammunition. In conclusion, they were one of best booties ships. We returned to Tunis after 33 days, every sailor took seven quintars and a half of sugar (one quintar=143.8 Kg), twelve broadcloth, and 125 rolls of silk. The sailing poles were fabricated with the strongest wood quality. They were solid and tall and can be used in the great ships. We decided to grant these poles to our glorious Sultan 'Salim Khan', we selected also 200 prisoners to send them with the poles. It was envisaged that 'Moheiddine Pieri Raiss' took her to Istanbul. Moheiddine was the nephew of the departed 'Kamal Raiss'. He was a perfect friend, savant, scientist knowing the Sultanate's ethics. Pieri Raiss left Tunis in a blessed hour seeking Istanbul.

# Chapter 14: Our Backbone Sultan

'Pieri Raiss' left Tunis in six sea pieces. He reached Istanbul in the day 21. He docked in facade of the coast 'Saray Borno' saluting the Sultan with cannon shells. The Sultan was pleased to receive Pieri Raiss, and he read personally my letter. He was satisfied and happy with what we accomplished, me and my brother Arruj of conquests. After he finished, he raised his two hands to the sky and make Dua (Allah Supplication) for both of us and our sailors.

He declared: "*Oh Allah, whiten the faces of your servants and slaves Arruj and Khaireddine in this life and the hereafter. Oh Allah, strike their haters, defeat their enemies, and grant them victory on land and sea*". That means we earn Sultan supplication and we will never be defeated. We became dear in both worlds (life and afterlife). About Pieri Raiss, he was privileged by the Sultan, he offered him twelve bags of Akja (Turkish coin) and he wears him with his generous hands the Sultanate's suit and we were honored by his acceptance of our gifts that we addressed to him and seeing them by himself one by one.

The Grand Sultan requested that the Pieri Raiss ships dock near the coast of his castle and this is an uncommon thing as it was never and ever any ship can anchor near his Highness'castle. Pieri Raiss ordered 200 prisoners to carry the gifts and stepping with them to the Sultan's castle. They walked with embroidered dresses in a military show in front of the Glorious Sultan, who awarded them every one with 50 dinars. Salim Khan specified Pieri Raiss with a wonderful residence. He ordered too the maintenance of the ships including their new painting and equipping them with the necessary. He also instructed the construction of two military ships, each one with 27 seats from the model 'Kaderga', which will be granted to me and for my brother Arruj. The sides of the two ships were decorated with a gold color and piled with shells which were light's shining as they were newly manufactured. Pieri Raiss visited too the ministers and delivered them their gifts addressed to them by us.

One day, the Sultan called him, he gave him two swords, each sword fist was studded with diamonds, the value of each one was equivalent to the amount of 'Rum' taxes (Spaniards, Venetians, Greeks, Bulgars, etc), he gave him too two Sultanate's dresses and two military badges. He directed him: *"Arruj rides one ship and Khaireddine the other. Arruj took a badge and a sword and, the same for Khaireddine, apprise them we accepted their gifts sent to us. I entrust you to Allah and ask him to perpetuate his victory over you and at any time if you have any need you can inform us to fulfill it"*. Pieri Raiss took the Sultanate's order like the orders his highness send to his officers, his ministers and his people, kiss it three times then put it on his head one time then he bent with respect seven times, finally he kissed the blessed hand of the Sultan and went out. Pieri Raiss rode one of the offered ships, ordered the rest to follow him, then salute the Sultan from the ship near 'Saray Borno' with eight sea pieces direction into Tunis.

In the time where Pieri Raiss was in Istanbul, I rode the sea me and my brother with ten boats destination to 'Sebta' strait (Ceuta today in Morocco mainland occupied by Spain) situated at the end of the Mediterranean as we will pass from there to AlAndalus to rescue as many as we can from our brothers in religion. In the meantime, it's coming to us a letter from Bejaya (in Algeria, same name until today) written on her: "*if there's a helper, it should be from you the heroic Mujahideen, we became incapable to do Salat (prayer) or teach our children the Quran from the great tyranny of the Spaniards, here we put our life between your hands. Allah makes us a cause for you to liberate us. You're welcome to come to our region and aid us.*"

When we were in the stage of sailing's intention to Berjaya, Pieri Raiss entered with his fleet. We welcomed him to our ship. We asked him eagerly about Istanbul news. When I saw his ship, I became astonished. She was immense and nicely decorated. When I read the Sultanate's letter, I became happier, my eyes with tears. I kissed the letter seven times and put it over my head and I thank Allah for making me a servant for a great Sultan like him. My brother Arruj reacted with extreme happiness like me and he supplicate Allah for the Sultan. The Salim Khan sent too a Sultanate letter to Tunis Sultan, I delivered it to him personally. After he kissed it seven times and put it over his head he opened it, it's written on it: "*To prince of Tunis, if my book* (letter) *reached you, you should work with its orders and be careful if not helping our servants Arruj and Khaireddine*".

In a big festivity with the presence of the Tunis Sultan, his officers and the crowds, Pieri Raiss gave us, me and my brother

Arruj, the two swords and the two military badges with also the two Sultanate's suits. The Tunis Sheikhs supplicated Allah for the Sultan Salim.

The Sultan of Tunis saw the exceptional care of the Sultan Salim Khan about us. He experienced considerable sympathy and honor, even the Sultans like him never reached it. His attitude changed, and he explained to me: "*your ways, you and your brother Arruj will result in the general Commandment of the Ottoman empire Navy. Congratulations to you*". From that note, the Tunis Sultan's perceiving of us became strange. He started telling us in contrary to what he had in his within as the envy settled in his heart. He became conscious that we were not yet just pirates without protection. We were under the glorious Sultan care and preservation. From that occasion, he struggled to avoid us and mistrust us, suspecting that we seize his kingdom for the grand Sultan Salim Khan.

# Chapter 15: A Counter Attack

The next day, I and my brother drove the two offered ships by Sultan 'Suleiman AlKanuni'(The Magnificent). Each Ship has 27 seats and 16 Cannons. We moved off in 12 sea pieces; On the way, we took over a ship full of wax carrying 25 Infidels imprisoning 40 from our Andalusian brothers. We liberated all of them and we sent them on a ship with 'Delly Mehmet Raiss' to 'Tunis'(capital of Tunisia, same name until today). I was always loving "Delly Mehmet Raiss". He was a brave young man who never knew the fear. If he dueled 15 to 20 lonely, he will defeat them. We came to the Algerian 'Bejaya' harbor in 2333 sailors, ten 'Kaderga' ships,150 Cannons, and thousands of captives that we lay them rowing.

The Infidels held the 'Bejaya' fortress. We clashed with them in a battle for three hours and a half. We got most of them. When 'AlBawadi Arabs' (individuals living outside Bejaya) heard about us, they came with 20000 men to help us, but most of them were unaware of the fight's arts. A bunch of kuffar (Infidels) barricaded themselves inside the fortress and they persevere in resistance for 29 days.

We were close to picking up the fortress. As we didn't have the right Cannons models adopted to bomb fortresses, this prevented us from generating enough wide holes in it. An information about a huge Spanish Force was advancing from the Minorca island on her pathway to us. We left 'Bejaya' pulling back to 'Jijel' (in Algeria too) to survey the Spaniards. Finally, ten Spanish 'Kaderga' model ships appeared on the horizon, full of weapons and military material. My brother Aruj said: " This is a grace Allah gave it to us". We attacked the Spanish ships with sailors, echoing the screams of praise. We collided with them in a tremendous battle ended by the capture of the ten Ships. Just 78 of the Spanish soldiers survived. We stuck them to the paddles to make them rowing.

# Chapter 16: The Spainish Enemy

We divided the Crusaders' banners over the ten Ships. I ordered 500 men to drive them and heading to 'Bejaya'. The Spaniards, who took refuge in the 'Bejaya' citadel, were waiting for the ten Spanish Ships to provide them with the supplies. When they looked at us, they supposed we were their religion's brothers. They raised their hats, waving them in the air, expressing their joy. This way we approach to the fortress sinking in his fake happiness. The kuffar opened the fortress gates, and they flocked to their coastal castles to receive the Ships arriving to their emergency. Suddenly, I instructed the sailors to quit to the coast. It shocked the Spaniards after they heard our screams. Fastly they returned defeated. We could open the fortress doors. Meanwhile, they shouted with terms like: "*Mina Senior*" appeal for the safety.

After the fortress conquer, the local people, including officials and the leaders of 'Bejaya' nearby, comes to make allegiance to me. From that date we became me and my brother Aruj kings in this region. I returned to 'Jijel' to meet him, after we seized 800 barrels of gunpowder and an infinite number of booties, we were glad especially with the gunpowder because we were near to be in out of stock and Tunis Sultan cut its supply for us and seems avoiding us day after day. We decided resolving our problems by ourselves. It became very necessary that we found a new country for us in our strangeness.

When the Spaniards heard about our conquest of 'Bejaya' fortress, they fell into a sea of sadness and sorrow. As a result, 'Carlos', the king of Spain, ordered 'Bejaya' liberation and the rescue of prisoners from Turks. In other side, the Algerians saw and felt that the Turks can divide the Spaniards Back. They are people of justice, fearing Allah (God). When I was in 'Jijel' with my brother, many delegations visited us from different Algerian cities. The most important ones were from Algiers, which was the Capital of the country (remark here that Algiers was already the Capital of Algeria from that era!)

The Algiers' inhabitants were suffering from the Spaniards' tyranny and they beg our intervention to protect them. As a reaction to their request, my brother Aruj took 500 men and headed to Algiers meanwhile I left 'Jijel' and aimed Tunis which its Sultan became a real enemy for us but when he saw me coming with ten ships, he feared about his throne and kingdom he expressed compliments on me and my brother and apologizing his lessening toward us. I asked him: *"What's the cause that forbid you to furnish us with the gunpowder*? He replied: *"I wasn't aware of your need for the gunpowder. My assistant didn't inform me about that and I ordered to cut his head because of that"*.

The Sultan has indeed ordered that, and he cut the head of his assistant but not for his misinformation about our need for gunpowder. It's for another cause. I didn't want to expose him, but I pretended to be convinced. We roamed together, me and the Sultan on our horses back to Tunis City, then I returned to 'Almarsa' (same name until today), we were together, me my oldest brother 'Isaaq Raiss', 'Mosleheddine Raiss', 'Kurd Oglo Raiss', 'Delly Mehmet Raiss' and others from the well-known sailors. I gave my orders to the Captains to sail to the Conquest in the east of the Mediterranean and 'Cyprus' surroundings (an island, same name until today) and then the return to Algiers. Meanwhile, I returned to Algiers with my brother, Isaaq.

The Captains took seven sea pieces and direction to the east. In their way, they coincide with the Ottoman fleet covering the sea, sailing between Cyprus and Egypt. The sailors expressed their happiness with this coincidence. 'Mosleheddine Raiss' approached in a fast speed the fleet then he boarded the 'Commandment ship' and stand up in front of Captain Daria (Navy level in Ottoman empire fleet), 'Jaafar Bey' (Bey is an official title used in Tunisia and Algeria until the first half of the twentieth century).

Who asked him: "*Don't you know the Sultan is in Egypt? Who forbid you from the participation in the 'Humayun'* (another name for the Sultanate's fleet) *Fleet*? 'Mosleheddine' was a wise man, he answered him: "*Sir, 'Maada Allah' (God forbid) that we neglect the service of the Sultan, as you know we are in a different region and we didn't have any awareness of what your honor says, if you sent any dog of yours* (he want to say any tiny information) *we could answer with high speed with complete obedience without delay, the service of the state is a great honor for us.*" The Captain Daria, 'Jaafar Bey' liked his method of answering, he said to him: "*God bless your mouth and Tongue*".

After that 'Mosleheddine' followed the Sultanate's fleet with the seven ships and he entered with him to Alexandria harbor. The Sultan 'Salim' was settling in Cairo after his conquest to Egypt. When he heard about his fleet in

Alexandria, he ordered its inspection! The Sultan honored 'Mosleheddine' and he gave him huge numbers of soldiers and military equipments, he took all this, then he returned to Algiers.

# Chapter 17: My Brother Triumph

My brother Arruj was intensely delighted after he knew how the Sultan 'Salim' reacted and his grant for the seven ships with soldiers and Cannons. I was in 'Jijel' when my brother Arruj was in Algiers City. We were already controlling a considerable part of the country. The Spaniards felt a major concern about that. Meanwhile, they were in the coastal garrisons. 40 sea pieces were prepared. Later they come to Tunis. They anchored in the 'Halk Alwadi' fortress. None was there. They didn't find anyone except us. When they discovered that, they know already, they'll fail to beat us, so they switch their armada to 'Algiers AlMarsa'. Their primary purpose was occupying the biggest harbor in Algiers Port from my brother, Arruj. Arruj spend that night praying to God, begging him to give him the Conquest.

At the Sunrise he assembled his sailors. He has a big number of mujahideen (Warriors) from Arabs, Berber and Andalusians, but they weren't specialists in the combat arts like the Turks. They were running away in the complicated situations. Their estimate was between 5000 to 6000. The enemy proceeded 10000 soldiers on the coast, the rest remained on the 40 ships.

My brother Arruj instructed that his flags raised up over the City towers and he arranged an aggressive military group to crush the invader. When the night shrouded the Place, he went out quietly from one of fortress doors with 3000 Warriors. He played a maneuver behind the ridges; he settled behind the Spaniards. It was a heavy black windy night. Allah conquers his servant mujahideen, meanwhile the Spaniards were suffering from these hard circumstances. They couldn't identify the movement of 'Arruj Raiss', who frightened them with a glance attack. They couldn't understand from where he issued this strike. He killed them all. The storm was accompanied by the fall of the hail, which was in the form of goose eggs! The Spaniards were massacring each other, petrified by this surprise. Then they took off the soldiers from the ships to the land. Their total was between 20000 to 30000 soldiers. The dark was profound. They couldn't see each other.Arruj Raiss continued his mass killing for them. It was a glorious Epic ended with the enemy's collapse. At the end of the night, another 2000 mujaheed went out of the citadel. They started too to annihilate the Spanish forces, oftenest massacred, and the rest were 2700 captives. Our Martyrs were 300, and we buried them with official ceremonies.

The Islam military won, the flag of Turks is raising and Spain conquered, which was regarded as the biggest infidel country in face of my brother Arruj and we set king Carlos' nose down in the mud. May Allah darken the infidels' faces. My brother Arruj wrote to me about this glorious triumph, when I received his letter, I was with my brother Isaaq arranging to move to Algiers with ten sea pieces to aid him but after this message we chose to leave for 'AlGhazw' (The Conquest), we took over in our sea road 16 kuffar ships packed with gunpowders, lead, wood, tar, oil, wheat and wheat. We returned to 'Jijel' after we spent 29 days in the sailing. I distributed a wheat ship to the poor from booties money. Later another book (letter) was sent to me by my brother Arruj instructing me to catch a crook Arabic Sheikh (Elder), instantly I took off with 500 men to the mountains where I arrested him and I ordered to cut his head and I designated another sheikh instead of him. After I took a breathing for several days, I rode the sea with over twenty ships. We attained the 'Algiers' harbor in a blessed hour. We unite me, Arruj and my bother Isaaq. We wasted a lot of time talking and arguing together. With this plan we pass all Winter season.

The Spring is here; the land is colored with all the various kinds of flowers; the ships left behind her anchors and turned, embracing the sea water. 'Tenis' City (west of the Capital Algiers, same name until today) was one of Algiers Places ruled by an Arab prince. This City was experiencing continuous troubles and disturbances, the locals tasted the insecurity from all that. That's why it was so simple for the Spaniards to control it. My brother, the Conqueror Arruj, thought of joining this city to his territories. In the meantime, Carlos, king of Spain, pretending the protection of 'Tenis' prince, addressed ten ships to the city, but his real objective is the revenge from the Muslims.

The prince of 'Tenis' possesses once a Spanish army division protecting him. This military division loot everything from the residents, then placed it on ships and sends it to Spain. My brothers Arruj and Isaaq settled in Algiers City, meanwhile I headed to 'Tenis' in ten ships. I coincided with my line four Spanish pieces docked in the harbor. The instant when they saw us, their hearts were extracted from their chests and they run away to the citadel seeking shelter inside it. We confiscated their ships, Cannons, and shooters that they left. For me I proceeded with 1500 man and I settled in facade of the fortress. I expected a tremendous defiance, but I discovered the fortress doors opened and some hundreds of Muslims exiting saluting us: "*You are welcome mujahideen, the Spaniards fled the fortress last night with their ally our prince, maybe they were 11000, they went out all of them including the prince's men, for the rest in the City they don't agree except for you and your brother the Sultan Arruj*".

Urgently, I moved 2000 soldiers behind the prince and the Spaniards. They trapped them in the next day, they roared at them: "*Where do you figure out you're evading for? You, the renegade Atheists, do you think you'll ride elsewhere from our hands*". After the fire shooting, they clashed together with the swords. The enemy could support our blades and our gunmen, which causes them dropping like the birds. The battle finished with imprisoning 350 from the kuffar, the rest of them the swords harvested them, meanwhile we lost 70 to 80 Martyrs may Allah make their seats in the Heaven. I received the Conquerors in the way of 'Tenis' fortress and I congratulate them on their triumph. Thus we lived for a while in "Tenis".

The share of the newest warriors in this Takeover was 500 Dinars but for the full spoils we got 150 Kayl (Weight unit of measure depending on the merchandise) of black pepper, 75 Kayl of Cinnamon and 25000 arm of cloth, the same for the Silk, 400 Kayl of Honey, 600 Kayl of Wax Honey, one thousand rolls of Wool beside a significant quantity of military machinery. I allowed a sailor's Chief as a governor on 'Tenis', therefore I rode the sea in a blessed hour with 16 ships to

Algiers City. When I met my relatives Arruj and Isaaq, we hold each other emotionally and the header of the Conquerors Arruj congratulates me saying: "*God bless your Conquests my brother*".

The 'Tenis' prince who rush away with the Spaniards was the nephew of the 'Telemsan' (same name until today) prince, didn't recognize what he earned from us, he was heard stating: "*Applauses for the Spain emperor, he will revenge for me from these Turks*". It became absolutely clear to us that this man doesn't carry in his soul any tiny thing from Islam. He thought the Spaniards were capable of taking Algiers from us and placing him as a Sultan on her. That way he was diving with his imagination in this delusion. Later, we were informed he occupied 'Tenis' with the support of Spaniards and some 'Bedouins' (desert residents) Besides this, the locals assumed he govern them again. My brother Arruj became furious he decided to walk to him personally, he gathered the Algiers Savants and asked them: "*What's the view of Islam for whom allied with the Spaniards who massacred and still slaughtering our brothers in religion and who rejected and still decline our advice?*" They acknowledged he must be executed. Then they wrote this 'Fatwa' (a certified religious judgement) and gave it to Arruj.

# Chapter 18 : A Traitor Fate

We goodbye our brother Arruj then he leave to 'Tenis'. When the 'Tenis' dwellers saw Arruj approaching the city, they perceived the danger of the threat, they captivated the nephew of Telemsan Sultan and released him to Arruj saying: *"You are the Sultan and we are your servants, the sin is from us and the tolerance is from you".* They continued talking with such hypocrite phrases. My brother Arruj was an emotional heart man. He hates the hypocrisy and the deception, tolerant and a pardoner that's why he offered his forgiveness to 'Tenis' Inhabitants. He invited their prince and he reproach him: *"What's up Bastard! What you made, no one, no one dare to do it before you! And I'll give no care about your rumors about me like I'm just a pirate who has no mission in this life just cutting the sea roads! Oh damned, you made yourself a slave to your enslaver, the monarch of Spain! Didn't you notice your king massacred hundreds of thousands of 'Andalus' (Spain) Muslims? We are not pirates but mujahideen we fight for the sake of Allah (God). Thanks to him".*

Then he directed the Executioner to cut the renegade's head. Later, He pressed the Arabs leaders telling them: *"You would grip this impostor from the beginning when he cames to you and sent him to me and what you performed after my coming can't negate your responsibility. Didn't you accept allegiance to me as Sultan upon you? How did you retire on your sworn?* Then he ordered to beat their necks too. When the 'Tenesians' saw all this, they affirmed the obedience to 'Arruj Raiss' as a Sultan upon them. My brother Arruj was aware that 'Telemsan' was the source of all the strifes and disturbs. She was a major metropolis on the extreme west near to 'Fass' (Morocco City Now, same name), also she was controlled by a royal family for a long time.

# Chapter 19: "Arruj Raiss" Death

The Sultan of 'Telemsan' was a miserable king and a subject to Spain's kuffar, for the locals they were suffering from both the Spaniards' oppression and their Sultan too. Long while ago, the 'Telemsanians' come to Arruj in Algiers City soliciting him to cut away this tyranny over them. My brother had the motive to occupy 'Telemsan' but she was long ly to the west near to 'Fass', furthermore she wasn't a seaside port and can't be reached with ships. Besides all this, the Sultan has a big army made up of Arabs and Spaniards. 'Telemsan' was the greatest province in Algeria and conquest her was certainly difficult. As long as 'Telemsan' was not freed, the entire Algeria will never recognize the stability.

In the meantime, the locals revolted against their Sultan and sent Elders to Arruj to swear loyalty to him to be their new Sultan. They contented my brother with this, as he wasn't obligated to struggle for this result. This devotion makes the Spaniards truly unpleased. It was the Spanish highest captain's 'Wahran' city (Oran: same name until now) Africa's resident that has the greatest harbor in the west of Algiers in the frontal of Spain. It carries too a gigantic citadel guarded by thousands of soldiers. 'Telemsan' was under the authority of Spaniards living in 'Wahran', when my brother Arruj became the

'Telemsan' governor, he ordered to cut all the relationships with 'Wahran'.

From another part, this captain own huge troops of soldiers and despite this he demanded further from Spain. My brother Arruj chose to spend the Winter in 'Telemsan' he posses 4000 fighters with him but he refused that the fortress of Algiers stay without guards, if Algiers go down, the full territory will be lost that's why he took with him just 1000 soldier. Arruj has arranged the plan of walking from 'Telemsan' to 'Wahran' in the Spring. When he was in 'Telemsan' and me in Algiers, he delivered to me 150 bags of silver money and 3000 sailors. It wasn't just the Spanish menace threating my brother but also the vanished Sultan from the City who gathered around him numerous bastards whose flocked to him for raiding and robbing, thus they wait for the event to make them slaying my brother.

This Sultan addressed to the infidel Captain in 'Wahran,' fortress motivating him and appealing to him to grant support for him notifying him: *"I fell in the hands of the Turks pirates and I couldn't get my wealth from them, so where is the glory and the strength of your monarch? Is that rationale that you can't even show your head fearing a negligible handful of Turks?* The Spanish Officer in 'Wahran' granted 20000 dinars to 'Telemsan' Sultan, and he learned to him he's forming an enormous army.

It was projected that this captain will move when the Spring settles with an Arabic-Spanish army to 'Telemsan' to confront my brother Arruj. Meanwhile, the Sultan himself gathered 20000 from the Berbers (Natives of North Africa). Promising them with different sorts of promises and appeals.

Later, another force joined him from 'Wahran'. Formed by 10000 soldiers. This army of 30000 fighters moved to 'Telemsan' headed by the Spanish Commander who was a truly arrogant dog.

My brother Arruj realized the futility of opposing these colossal forces in an open area. He directed the City evacuation once he took protection in the rampart. The kuffar entered 'Telemsan', committed unbelievable crimes, then they besieged the fortress. I was in Algiers. I knew about the degradation of the situations. I prepared 1000 Turkish guards and 2000 Arabic Knights and placed them under the command of my brother 'Isaaq Raiss' and I solicited him to displace the sooner to our brother Arruj to aid him. My bother 'Isaaq Raiss' moves with this full force beside his assistant 'Iskander Raiss'. When my brother Arruj received this message, he goes out from the citadel to join with Isaaq their forces.

The City dropped in the grips of the Sultan, and the two forces were unified. Arruj started thinking of a potential solution. The Sultan of 'Telemsan' was the last one in his aristocratic family that ruled the City for hundreds of years ago and indeed she dominated the entire Algeria. For this reason, my brother Arruj wouldn't deprive this family of her throne and its influence. He would prefer that she broke her alliance with the Spaniards and agree to remain in our supreme state. If she rejects these two conditions, we will be compelled to omit it from the existence.

My brother came back to 'Telemsan' with 2000 soldiers. 10000 Arabs and Spaniards confronted him. The two forces clashed together in a harsh battle during for three hours and a half, swords covered with bloods and finished by the bloodshed of most of the Infidels. We just saved 300 or 400 from them got as hostages to Algiers. The Spain king 'Carlos' issued a Farmen to his governor in Wahran ordering him: "If you want to keep your head, you must kill Arruj Raiss and all the Turks with him or you must send me Arruj alive to Spain and I know the manner that I'll execute him with". Upon this Farmen, it occurs great battles later, between the two sides for three months.

Despite the significant difference in the number of soldiers, my brother Arruj never concede for them. He fights with his sons as invincible. Something pushed the 'Wahran,' governor to express his army's Commanders: "*Those Turks are very determined people they are extremely resistant they'll don't abandon even they were massacred to the last one, for how long time we will stay under the walls of this Castle? Let's addressing them a Messenger telling them they grant us the citadel. In counter-part, they grabbed their weapons and their necessities with safety. They'll accept this if their supplies end. If the supplies remain, they will never submit until the death of the last man*".

In the next morning, the Mediator met my brother Arruj. After this encounter, my brother Arruj asked the presents: "*What do you suggest, sons? You listened to the Messenger*". The soldiers said: "*Sure life is better than death. Let's depart from Algiers. Later, we'll come back to re-pick up the Castle again. This is our view, but the last word is for you, you're wiser than us*". Arruj accepted to provide the Castle to the Spaniards, whose became very joyful as they have a concealed intention than the deal. They have the aim of killing Arruj and his troopers when they move. If the king Carlos know they left them alive, he would hit the neck of 'Wahran' governor. Arruj left with his guys, whose were between exhausted and hungers after a protracted span of confrontation without pause and feed beside the completion of their arms and ammunitions.

After they walked for a slight distance, a Spanish force made up of 15000 to 20000 soldiers caught them up. The Commandant of the group told them: "*Drop your weapons, is not sufficient that you pass safe?*" Arruj answered him: "*Death is righter than leaving the weapons. Who is the death itself that we worry it? The man die one time but his name still eternal*". A discouraging battle begun. My brother was killing anyone who came to him from the kuffar, but in every round several Martyrs fell as the Turks number was not over than 340 soldiers. With his companions, they arrived in a river he has the intention of throwing himself on it, the half of Turks crossed the river but the Spaniards could catch them up.

My brother couldn't resist to the screaming of his soldiers asking for his help. He loves them like a father does with his children; he returned to them. The wise requested that he and the passed soldiers continues to Algiers, then he'll come back after he restore his powers to revenge his brothers, but the Turks sailors were calling him: 'Baba' (Father), a father can't leave his children dies under the swords while observing them without reaction.

Arruj returned to the bridge, and he threw himself into the Spaniards, getting the maximum of them. They exhausted the sailors. Even one of them couldn't carry the sword with his hand. All this was in a heated day, it split even their lips from the thirst. My brother killed almost one hundred Spaniards before he fell Martyr, then they cut his blessed head and sent it to the king Carlos. My brother Isaaq was Martyr months earlier in the Castle of the all Castles!

We were four brothers. I experienced and suffered the Martyrdom of three. How is it great the wisdom of Allah! I'm the only one who is not Martyr! That's mean my three brothers are better than me for Allah (God). May Allah put them all in paradise. Amen By the sanctity of the Prophet Muhammad, may God bless him and grant him peace. When I knew about my brother's death; I decided to follow the same path that he thrived on. This point was regulating the presence of the Spaniards in Africa and in the Mediterranean sea. What's the purpose of living after my brother's death! It wasn't the occasion to show the character of fear and fragility; we didn't have time to cry as we are just a handful of Turks in Africa! They could finish us in a blink of an eye. I took many precautions and measures, but the enemy couldn't find a power to push him to come to Algiers.

I spent that Winter preparing, and I didn't allow to myself any moment to avoid thinking about my brother Arruj. But every night I saw him, I wake up and the sadness full my heart. I was focusing in the work to forget; I renewed all the ships, the Cannons and the equipments. The Spaniards were saying: *"The thanks for Jesus, he relieved us of the biggest calamity and now we must finish the little one before converting the snake into a dragon."* It comes to me a Messenger from Spain king telling me: *"Your brother killed, the same for the most of his soldiers, we broke your wing, who do you think yourself to stand up in front of the most powerful Christian king without your brother? What can you do? Take your ships and soldiers and leave Algiers immediately and never rethink, to put your foot in Africa again.*

*This is the last warning for you. I'll fulfill the sea with ships and I'll return to Algiers sooner. If I'll catch you there, be sure your end will be very sad."*

I was the Sultan of Algiers and I was a simple servant for the Ottomans with an official title 'Baylar Bey' of Algiers, but the Europeans knows me with the name of 'Algiers king' and when the king of Spain talked to me with this disparagement, I wrote to him a hard speech. When he received it, he sent fleets covering the horizon, taking part in, the kings of Naples, Sicily, Germany, Netherlands and Belgium, who were subject to Carlos.

Their ships anchored near to Algiers, they descended their forces to the land. I was adequately supplied for Winter; I expected his reaction. That's why when they get off to the beach, we set our swords on a vast number of them, meanwhile 700 to 800 infidels from 20000 surrendered, the rest ran away to their ships. The Carlos' followers' kings returned shamefully after their noses merged in the defeat's dirt.

The result of this battle was the rise of the Turks' reputation in Africa and we became famous in the entire Europe. It was 13000 prisoners in Algiers, 24 from them were high level Captains known for Europeans as 'Admirals'. Controlling them was a hard task, on an occasion, they broke their chains and escaped. We couldn't capture and controlling them again only after a strong battle and the death of 300 from them. I instructed the mintage and the 'Friday Prayer Speech' (Friday Prayer every week for Muslims worldwide) in the name of Sultan 'Salim Khan'.

My purpose was the mintage and the 'Friday Prayer Speech' can't be done in the name of another Sultan except the Greatest

Ottoman Sultan "Salim Khan". At this stage, the Sultan of Morocco was considered the ultimate Arabic Sultan in Africa. I concluded that if the Morocco Sultan subjugation for Turks is not completed, it will never be for the entire Africa. One day I invited several Arabs princes to an assembly, and I explained them: "*The Sultan Salim Khan is 'The Khalifa' of the prophet Muhammad Peace and Blessings be upon him (he represents him in Muslims), how do you leave 'The Khalifa' of the Muslims and the world Sultan and you do mintage and the 'Friday Prayer Speech' in the name of Morocco Sultan? Your fate and the future of your people depend on the mintage with the identity of the Greatest Sultan. Woe to you if you disobey*".

I sent 'Hajji Hussein Agha' who was my trusty man to my Sir the Sultan 'Salim Khan'. After sea travel of 21 days, he landed at the pearl of the sea 'Istanbul'. The Sultan received him in his coastal Palace. 'Hussein Agha' put in the hands of his greatness the modest gifts that I sent to him. Twenty European boys carried the gifts. The Sultan, with his gentleness, accepted her and he declare his appreciation for her. The Sultan wore 'Hussein Agha' the Sultanate's suit, and he directed to honor my Captains and placing them in the 'Amiri' (Princes) guest houses. After his visit to the Sultan, 'Hussein Agha' visited the other divisions of the state and offering them the humble gifts I addressed to them. 'Agha' stood in the City of 'The world Throne', Istanbul. 41 days passed by my Captains in eating, drinking and relaxation. When the date for their leave is coming, the Sultan ordered that the Algerian ships pass near his coastal Palace to watch her.

The ships performed a show with Cannons' shells. Before he left Istanbul, 'Agha' went on a last visit to the Sultan, when he entered to his greatness, he kissed the ground in front of him seven times, the Sultan granted him a Farman written by his own hands containing my designation as 'Baylar Bey' over Algeria, formerly he gave him a sword studded with diamonds, a golden tailored dress and the Ottoman flag and he instructed him: "*Listen 'Raiss', bring this sword to Khaireddine Basha* (Barbarossa), *he wear the Sultanate's suit and he rise always my flag, I ask Allah to make you always conquerors and whiten your faces in both the houses* (life and afterlife). *Amen by the Sanctity of prophet Muhammad Peace and Blessings be Upon him.*"

After he left Istanbul, 'Agha' docked his ships in 'Corone' harbor in south of Almora (Liguria in Italy today). It was eight sea pieces tied up in the harbor belonging to the Venetians and with an infinite number of Turkish ships. 'Hussein Agha' did a courtesy visit to an Admiral of the Venetian's ships and he advised him: "*Algeria became subject to Sultan Salim and my sir Khaireddine Basha an Ottoman 'Beyler Bey' on her. Also, our fleet became a section of the Ottoman fleets. For this, we will operate under the orders arriving from Istanbul. If you are friends to our Sultan, no fear about you from Algeria ships but if you are enemies for him, we will forbid you from the sailing in the sea*".

After eight days of leaving 'Corone' harbor, 'Hussein Agha' reached Algiers. That way, his trip from Istanbul to Algiers endure 16 days. I invited immediately 'Agha' and the Commanders. When he arrived in front of me I got the gifts with great glorification and profound appreciation, I kissed her and placed her over my head then I set the sword in his place, I wore the Sultanate suit and I placed the Ottoman flag in a high position near me. I felt great comfort for myself. The Spaniards will never annoy me after this day because the greatest Sultan 'Salim Khan' supports me in my back.

Everything I need, he will afford it with his generosity and his care. At that night I did a great festivity and I honor 'Hussein Agha' as he did his mission perfectly and I assigned him to a top official position in Algiers. There's no doubt that our biggest enemies are the kuffar of Spain also we were in a war state with others like the Venetians but from our first settling in Algeria we were in a continuous preoccupation with the local princes from Algeria, Tunis and Morocco as they were not pleased that we are here. The Morocco king, for example, he's a descendant of a great royal family that wastes her authority and her influence in the last period because of the internal wars and there wasn't in north Africa any relevant country except the Morocco.

For 'Tunis' and 'Telemsan', which were ruled by 'Alhafssiun' and 'Beni Abdel wadi', they didn't eventually have any influence. The Sultans and princes of Tunis and Telemsan began making partnership with Spanish kuffar and plotting against us implicitly and deliberately. They already realize that we will finish them at the first opportunity. Why? I'll explain that. When we were moving from the east of the Mediterranean sea, we settle on Tunis after an arrangement with her Sultan.

Thanks to us, the Tunisian economy flourished and the Tunisian Cities enriched after she was in ruins and Tunis inhabitants lives in prosperity. Thanks to us too, the Tunis Sultan gets rid of Spanish control and his treasury became full of money because of taxes that we pay for him. We were glad for him and Allah (God) testify that never we had any wrong intentions towards him, his kingdom and his wealth! If we wanted, we would do it in so many opportunities, but we didn't. In these conditions, we conquered Algeria. As a result, we gained a land bigger than Tunis and we started an unfinished war with the strongest Christian country.

Based on Islam teaches the Tunis Sultan should associate with us, but he was doubting, especially when we became under the Ottomans. What we recognize the Ottomans are a family governing a world's country and 'Salim Khan' annexed in just several years kingdoms bigger than Tunis one hundred's time. Sultan 'Tunis' thought that our glorious Sultan 'Salim Khan' was in greed for his poor kingdom! He forgot that the 'Beylar Beys' of our Sultan owns large fertile lands bigger than lands in 'Tunis' and they have military brigades bigger than his own.

That way, the gap between us and Tunis Sultan became further expanded. He wasn't able to confront me lonely, so he seeks help from the Spaniards sometimes and he tries to revolute the local princes against me in other time. The one who acted to his appeals was the Sultan of "Telemsan" isolated from "Alzayanine" family throne. This Sultan was under my rule but he was consistently working to associate with Spaniards secretly and the letter addressed to him by Tunis Sultan fell in my hands. This is the resume of this message: *"This called Khaireddine is unusually strong. He's even more dangerous than his brother 'Arruj'. He's backed now by the Sultan "Salim Khan" so there're no limits to his arrogance.He stuck in his head seeking for a world country including Spain itself! Sultan Salim thinks Khaireddine is undoubtedly a man of state! He made him a "Beylar Bey" and "Basha" and he gave him the studded sword, the Sultanate's suit and the Ottoman flag and he allowed him to gather from Alanadhool his lacks in men, weapons and military materials. The best for all of us. We must be on one hand and we shouldn't leave any Turk in north Africa. In just ten years after their first entrance, they became our lords!*

# Chapter 20: The Ottomans Power

The all things are for Allah! He honors whom he wills and humiliates whomever he wills. 'Tunis' Sultan was blind to that and because of his mistakes and various sins, Allah humiliated him. Now, Algiers is under my rule and no human force can get it from me because this land is not my property, but it's for our greatest Sultan 'Salim Khan'. Until today, none heard that a country was taken from the Ottomans. This is the fact that must be recognized. Anyone who rejects it he deserves the consequences. The Algiers inhabitants love us and they felt truly the grace that they live in. From our coming to their motherland, we could unite so many tribes in this vast country.

The trading prospered so many times and the Muslims felt protected from the Spaniards' persecution and became free. Their heads are up. All this because they were followers of the greatest Sultan. Despite all this, some tribes reacted to 'Tunis' Sultan incitements. I sent them a force composed of 6000 men and 6000 Knights. These tribes have been disciplined. For the 'Telemsan' Sultan, he was plotting with the Morocco Sultan. Meantime, the 'Telemsan' citizens were deeply unstable because of the throne fights inside the royal family 'Alzayanine', meanwhile the Spaniards were amused watching what develops in 'Telemsan'.

One day, a prince from Alzayanine family arrives to Algiers seeking asylum and help against his old brother. I sent with him a force constitute 3000 knights and 1000 walkers to 'Telemsan'. My decision was based upon my spies information, revealing that the Sultan 'Mawlai Abdellah' started provoking people against us and slag us. This Sultan that we save from the Spaniards' tyranny must be punished for his ingratitude and expressing his enmity to us. Like that, when he heard about the arrival of our forces, he run away to 'Wahran' seeking help from the Spaniards.

# Chapter 21: Telemsan City

The Notables of 'Telemsan' abandoned their Sultan declaring their complete autonomy from him saying: "The Prince 'Massoud' came with a dominant force sent by 'Khaireddine', do whatever you do and think how to act. It's not our dilemma. The Sultan recognized he was in a grave situation and he couldn't find any solution than take refuge in the Spaniards. The prince 'Massoud' won a cold fight with no drop of blood. Thanks to us, he entered 'Telemsan' and sit on her throne.

He claimed a lot of Dua (Supplication) for us. We wouldn't trust him after he attained his target. He rewarded my soldiers; gave everyone 25 golden dinars, and he compensated too, the Arabic Volunteers coming with him to fight, 10 golden dinars but for me he sent 50000 golden dinars the annual taxes amount beside a great number of valued gifts reflecting his gratitude. I sent the gold to the Algiers' treasury. I shared most of the gifts to the sea Captains and I conserve some of them in my Palace.

Then I addressed a paper to the Sultan 'Massoud' advising him: *"Now thanks to our Sultanate you sit on your ancestors' throne, be conscious of the cause that forbids your brother from his throne. Don't harass the Muslims and don't infringe my orders and never delay the payment of the annual taxes a single day.*

*Never hearing about a potential relationship between you and the Spaniards, whose will finish you the day when they overcome you. Remember, your two oldest brothers are refugees with the Spaniards and if you wish no longer see one of them on your throne, get the preconditions for that".*

But 'Massoud' from the moment of sitting on his throne, he started oppressing people and took their money as his ancestors did for a long time ago. I knew that when he read my letter he rip it into pieces. He was oblivious to what he waiting for his doing. His oldest brother in 'Wahran' heard about what he did. He contacted me stating: *'Sir the Sultan, didn't you understand how you remove me from my forefathers' throne? And you put in my place an ungrateful one who never appreciated your grace on him. He's against you now. If you are pleased to make me get back my throne, I'll be a faithful servant for you and your sultanate forever".*

We didn't expect the good from this one as we didn't from his brother 'Massoud' but the politics require now that we grant him amnesty to strike his brother 'Massoud' with him. In this meantime, I was anchoring with 22 ships in 'Mostaganem' harbor (same name until now) which I seized it without trouble. 'Mostaganem' was very close to 'Wahran' that was in the Spaniards' hands. When I was in 'Mustaghanem' it came to me, the prince 'Abdallah'. He kissed my suit with begging. I sent with him 1000 men to 'Telemsan'. For me, I was preoccupied by the inhabitance of 2285 immigrant Andalusian in 'Mustaghanem' areas. I transported them to my ships from Spain. I afforded them lands living and working on her. They were professional workers. Everyone has a well mastered specific competence.

# Chapter 22: A Trap

I knew that 'Abdallah' arrived in 'Telemsan' and became the governor. Meanwhile, his brother seek protection in the Castle for 25 days. The sailors realize that the siege will take a long duration as they don't have the specific Cannons that can be used with castles'attacks. They argued together, and they expressed: *"Let's finish the siege and pretending to run away, those 'Bedouins' has no experience and can't discern between the victory and the defeat, they'll spread between them that the Turks are escaping and their eager to the booties will make them following us, thus we beat them, seizing the Castle, give it to prince 'Abdallah' and later we return to Algiers"*. And this happened. The 'Massoud'supporters went out from the Castle crying: *"Look to these Turks, they run away"*. They followed the sailors, whose counter-attack them, killing most of them.

Those 'Arabs' (another designation to Bedouins or the desert inhabitants) ignore the arts of war and they consider that the fight of the regular Armies is like the looting in the desert. The Spaniards, whose learning the arts of war, savored for so many times the pain of the defeat. If those 'Bedouins' have a mind, they would never risk their lives for free. They didn't have any care for the human soul! They expose themselves to the death stupidly and they think that this is Allah's decree and destiny! In reality, there are some of them were courageous knights, but their rode of the horse was remarkably primitive. Besides that, they didn't own suitable weapon, even if it exists they can't operate it well! They didn't retain effective firearms.

The primary cause for their failure is that they don't work with the 'collective' fight strategy. There's no coherence between their actions. That way the 'Telemsan' Castle fell in the hands of the sailors, meanwhile the Sultan 'Massoud' disappeared with five or ten from his fellows without a trace. None knows about their fate. This is the consequence for whom has no mind. So who is this 'Massoud' to defy me? I'm the 'Beylar Bey', one of the greatest Sultans in the world! And he sees that me and my brother Arruj, we defeated the Spain king on several occasions. This traitor 'Massoud' abandoned 6000 Bedouins in the Castle without being informed. Even they were persistent in fighting against my sailors, ignoring that their leader left before conceding.

Their Leaders told my sailors: "*Maada Allah (God Forbid) that we were voluntary to disobedience of Algiers' Sultan Khaireddine Basha (Barbarossa), he is our Master and the Turks are our parents, what should we do? We rise the weapons in front of their faces, worrying from the Spaniards that 'Massoud' threatened us with. So many of us took part in many Conquests with 'Arruj Raiss'. Forgive us, the evil is from us and from you the pardon and the generosity*". In his battle, my sailors killed 5000 bedouins and tolerated who left their weapons and declared their surrendering. And on the day of Friday, the prayer speech was told in the name of our Sultan 'Salim Khan' and they stamped his name on the coin. The sailors saluted the Sultan 'Abdallah' and requested approval to leave to Algiers, but he begged them remaining for a while. They inform him they didn't have orders to stay after the Castle Conquest.

After he insisted on them, they agreed to allow 100 of them with him. The Sultan took a considerable care of my sailors; he offers them the same food that he eats. The rest 900 returned to Algiers with 20000 dinars and so many gifts. I read the letter assigned by 'Abdallah' and I found that it's written in a very polite style. I spoke to my sailors, smiling: *"He's now communicate with the appropriate way, we will see what he will do after he settles over his throne. Do will he follows his brother's path?"*

The Captains laughed for that, meanwhile I started thinking to search a solution for the problem of 'Ibn Alkadhi' after I closed the 'Telemsan' one. 'Ibn Alkadhi' was one of well known Arabs in Algeria. He appreciates me and has deep respect for me. The 'Tunis' Sultan tried to incite him against me but he refused and encouraged him to stay under the Ottoman's reign, not the Spaniards' one.

This rational father is dead now, and his son who bears the same name too 'Ibn Alkadhi' succeeded him, but this boy is not like his father, he's unwise boy. The first thing that he made, he stand side by side with the Sultan of 'Tunis' against me and he suggested to him: *"Let's be on one hand and force the Turks leave the land of Arabs"*. The letter that he sent to this Sultan fell in my hands and that before the pass of two months after his father's death. Some phrases in this letter: *"We should evict Khaireddine from Algeria, then I'll be the new Sultan and I'll spoil you with a lot of money. My father was Turks lover but for me I hate them"*. After this letter I was convinced that they plotting against me. I went out to 'Tunis' with 12000 men and

I descended on a plain covered with the oak and chestnut trees. When the Sultan of 'Tunis' saw me from a distance, he thought that I'm his associate 'Ibn Alkadhi'. I bombarded him with a rain of shells, causing his forces to disperse like knot beads. The Sultan imprisoned, and they brought him to me. I didn't mind advising him and warning him if he do this again. Later I released him.

I already know that he would kill me savagely if I was in his place, but my mercy for him and my pleasant treat make the locals respect us further and respect better the Turks. In this battle, I seized 300 tents I ordered to be delivered to Algiers. Then I resided in this field for five to ten days. The place was very wonderful, the small rivers were dispersed here and there, the birds sings with charming tones. We enjoyed ourselves for a period of times at that place. Then I called for the move to Algiers. We were walking in a mountain's small way, it can pass just one human. In the meantime, 'Ibn Alkadhi' prepared us for a trap. We just waked up when they attacked us from all directions. I didn't foresee that we dropped into this trap. In that state, with the difficulty of moving beside the massive surprise, I lose many of my men. The battle took three hours and a half, then we could cross the road and we could arrive at Algiers.750 sailors fell Martyrs in this battle. Because of that, I swore to revenge on this traitor and I'll never forgive him.

It was a God's destiny as I defeated the sultan of 'Tunis'and detained him and I didn't overcome a Bedouin like 'Ibn Alkadhi'. In the time when the Europeans heard my name, they shivering, the disobedience movement was expanding in Algeria. The arrogance of 'Ibn Alkadhi' grows day after day until he could express openly: "*I conquered 'Khaireddine Basha' and nearly I'll break his neck*".

I was informed that he brought together a great number of Arabs around him, and he imprisoned 500 Turks. They attached them with the heavy chains; he tied them to wheat mill and force them revolving around it like the beasts do. I wrote to him to release them or he will regret that. He didn't respond for a while, but later, he told me he will never allow them going because they'll avenge him after their liberation. On another hand, he sent to different Algeria areas inviting people to disobedience saying: "*Why the Turks are coming to Algiers? This is the land of Arabs. Let's unite our forces and finish them once*".

# Chapter 23: The Traitor

At that stage, I have 12000 Turkish sailors. Most of them are in the sea. It was mandatory that I expect any sudden attack from the Christians. That's why I couldn't apt to gather all my men and dispatch them to suppressing the rebels. In these circumstances, some Turks who lives with us imagined I can't handle Algeria governing and I'll lose her. One of these sailors, a young called 'Kara Hasan'. He thought he can revolute against me and sit in my place and his little mind told him he can do what I wasn't able to do.

When I discovered his messaging 'Ibn Alkadhi', I expelled him. I felt a state of apathy and I said I should give the Algeria inhabitants a painful lesson that they'll never forget it. 'Ibn Alkadhi' was eager to be Sultanate over Algeria but if I left Algeria, she will be divided into one thousand parts, each one of these parts will be held by the Spaniards one after one. 'Ibn Alkadhi' hasn't the ability to preserve the stability, neither he has the mind and the courage, neither the troops making him pushing the Spaniards. Not just that, he didn't even have a flotilla or a single ship. When the kuffar fleets fill up the horizon, how will he rise his head? Before our settling in Algeria, when they saw the Spanish ships, they disperse like the flocks of fowl.

For over one hundred years, it was never a state or government in Algeria. The infidels were aware of that, that's why they seized the best Algerian harbors. Now all what we established is risked to be destroyed because of a handful of madmen. The growth in trading and economy occurred will be gone the day when we leave Algeria, but the little mind people were ignoring this truth.

I planned to quit Algiers for a term to an outlying place occupying myself with the piracy and don't be involved in the land affairs and I'll see how the Algerians will manage their lives and secure their power and how they'll defend their region. I was sure that they'll do what they did exactly years ago, they'll send a messenger to me asking me to come back to Algiers. Then I'll return and nobody can push me to leave her again forever and they'll recognize that the state governance and administration is a skill specified for the Turks.

# Chapter 24: "Ibn Alkadhi" War

At the end, the storm started and 'Ibn Alkadhi' attacked me with 40000 men's army. I was prepared for it as I expected it before. Beside I had my spies on the council of 'Alkadhi' himself, all what was told and projected to be done, I was informed about it step after step. I sent 10000 sailors to push the rebellions. They collided with them in a terrible battle ended the afternoon. I lose in this battle 2000 Martyrs and 2000 wounded, but the battle finished by the rioters' defeat except for 700 whose escaped, for the rest they were jailed or killed. One of the detained was their chief, 'Algiers Sheikh' (An Elder with an official grade). I ordered his execution and his body was divided into four pieces and put each portion on a door of City's wall doors. After the elimination of the strife, I assembled 185 leaders who were behind it, chained, and I welcomed the Savants of Algiers. I told them: "*Our Masters, what's the punishment about these captives in our religion?*" One of them who was an aged one replied: "*The judgment for whom fighting you and your soldiers in Islam is the death, because you represent in this area the king of land and sea our Sultan 'Salim Khan'. You are the prince of his princes. Beside you were a good cause to prosper our daily lives and economy, you protect us from the tyranny of the Spaniards and we recognize in your era and the era of your brother Arruj, Allah grant him the mercy, an efficient*

*administration and supervision for the Muslims affairs something we were never seen it before. And now these 185 miserable were deceived by illusions of the governing. They did a colossal crime, but there's between them whose fought against the Spanish kuffar when they were with Arruj. Today, they make a mistake if there's a space for pardon, grant them amnesty, accept their apologize and utilize them in your favor. The pardon is the eye of honor and chivalry".*

I asked the present sea Captains: "*And you, what do you see?*" One of Captains answered: "*Sir the Basha, you're more aware than us we are not a religion Savants we are just warriors responsible in the front of the glorious Sultan in Istanbul and we are obliged that our actions are built on this principle, this is not the moment of amnesty and kindness. What they'll do these traitors if we were in their places? They recognized their crime. If we tolerated them, this will be an awful example for others. We are the Turks. We are just a handful dispersed in a territory bigger in number of times than Alanadhool* (part of Turkey) *trying to handle it with several thousands, in the same time we fight Spain, which is the biggest country in Europe. I see that you beat their necks to be an excellent lesson for others.*"

# Chapter 25: Leaving The Town

It came out to me what one of my sailors' Captains said is the appropriate judgment. I directed to cut the heads of the criminals' leaders without touching their money or properties. At that night I couldn't sleep; I was unhappy to take this decision as so many of them fought with my brother Arruj in the past, but the state protection required this decision. This immense country, we can't rule it in the harsh way, but with this hard decision we put fear in so many hearts even not forever, but at least for a while.

For a long time, I was studying to quit Algiers after these revolts, in the same time I know the locals loves us and if we leave them, certainly the Arabs will not succeed in its governance, beside their failure to fight the Spaniards our retreat will influence hardly the commerce and trading benefits for the all. I haven't any doubt that the Arabs will fight each other and never can be unified after my leave. The locals will encounter great harm as a result of that, thus they'll can't identify any solution for these issues unless they call for this from me. I was confident of that as my trust in my faith and beliefs. At that night I saw 'Elkhedher' peace be upon him in a dream (in Islam theology, an immortal prophet along the human history lived even in Soleiman and David prophets eras), I became optimistic and I felt like it was an excellent decision. One morning I carried my sailors and their families in my 25 ships anchored in the harbor and I addressed to my ships which were in the large of sea or in the Conquest (AlGazw) to lead to 'Jijel' harbor instead of Algiers'.

The locals flooded to the harbor. They thought we'll move out to the Conquest in Spain coasts, but when they saw we brought our spouses and money to the ships, they were shocked and so many of them depressed and fell in sadness.

After a one day travel, we arrived at Jijel's beautiful harbor. 'Jijel' was the first Castle I conquest with my brother 'Arruj Raiss'. When the locals of 'Jijel' knew about our return, they were extremely content. They performed a big festivity to welcome us as now, all the money and fortunes which flowed to Algiers in the past, will go now to 'Jijel'. In the next day crowds of people and elders coming from 'Jijel', 'Algiers' and even 'Tunis' were coming to assert on devotion to our Sultan 'Suleiman Khan' and they listen and obey for his orders. Later they present me the annual taxes and inform me they are ready to afford me with the men and all the urgent needs and announcing: *"Maada Allah* (God forbid) *that we defy our Sultan Suleiman Khan, we haven't any relationship with that, we are proud of our allegiance to Suleiman Khan"*.

I remained for a little in 'Jijel' I went out to 'Alghazw' (Conquest), I entered to Sicily island coasts (in Italy) and I bombarded 'Palermo'. In meantime I caught nine sea pieces from kuffar's ships which were carrying 40 storeroom full of wheat, barley, olive, olive oil, wood, dry beard, rice, coffee, silk and lead. I built in 'Jijel' several military camps and houses and I sold 36000 keyl (weight unit of measure) of wheat with very cheap prices for bakers, also I established a small factory for the ships' construction. In the same Summer, another time, I sent my ships for the Conquest. I vise Venice gulf where I seized three ships. Each one was carrying 10000 pieces of gold beside hundreds of hostages. It was between them 60 Muslim prisoners I ordered instantly to liberate them. This Conquest dures 23 days.

In the day 24, my ships docked in 'Jijel' harbor, I directed to distribute a ship load for the poor and selling the other ships' goods. The proportion for every sailor was 125 gold piece, four shooters, five guns and eight kantar (one kantar is 143.8 kg) and a half from iron and 17 roll of Venetian cloth with another 225 cloth roll. The spoils were absolutely massive. Something drove the merchants rushed to purchase it. For me, I made to myself a ship with 26 paddles. She was big and speed. I placed her in a ship's race she won. In the cold, we retired all the ships to the land. When the Spring comes, we set up their maintenance, painting and equips them. Then I move out to the Conquest in 15 pieces.

I entered firstly to Genoa gulf; I spent 14 days bombing its coasts. I captured in that period 21 ships, I ordered to be shipped to 'Jijel'. After that, I over-passed the strait of 'Massina' (between Sicily and Italy mainland, same name until now). Then I entered the gulf of Venice. I detected a small flotilla of three ships sailing like the arrow escaping from us.

I followed the flotilla until I captivated it. I discovered they were the ships of 'Sinan Raiss' who rode my ship, kissed my hand and cry from the joy. It ran long time we didn't meet together. Then he accompanied me until we exit Venice gulf. We seized in the meantime another nine kuffar ships. That state the sum of the captured ships became 30. Some ships were charged with wheat, others with honey, some with cloth, and some with pepper. Another one was stuffed with warriors.

# Chapter 26: Turmoils In Algiers

In the meantime, 'Kurd Oglo Raiss', one of my Captains arrived in 'Jijel' with three ships. He offered me 10000 golden piece I forwarded them to the state coffer. At these days, each week, one of my Captains came with seized kuffar ships to 'Jijel' harbor. Meantime, the delegations came one after another from Algiers. The locals recognized our value in a short period after we left the City. The City is no longer secure and the troubles are in recurrence. As a repercussion, the sentiments of complaining are increasing against 'Ibn Alkadhi'.

At the end, the citizens formed a special commission to dialogue with him: "*We judge that inviting 'Khaireddine Basha'* (Barbarossa) *to our place will produce abundance for all of us. He was perfect in a manner that he retired from the City to leave the people survive in safety and harmony. Does existed anyone acted like him before? We came for you praying that you accept the return of 'Khaireddine' again and you leave for your tribe.*" He retorted to them: "*Oh fools! Don't you remark that 'Khaireddine' left the City fearing of me?* 'Kara Hasan' who was my sailor that I expelled him as he pondered to take my place before, didn't support what 'Ibn Alkadhi' stated and he reacted saying him: "*My Sultan, 'Kaireddine' that I perceive don't fear just from Allah (God), don't think that he left the City fearing from this or from that, he did this for something in his within but undoubtedly he didn't quit the City fearing you."* This speech makes 'Ibn Alkadhi' furious, but he didn't reveal this to 'Kara Hasan'. Instead, he ordered directly to cut the head of the delegation leader who suggested to him my invitation to the Capital.

This leader was an Arabic Religion's Savant. These events were giving the impression of our imminent return to Algiers. Despite this, we would wait until things roll like we prefer as the impress of 'Ibn Alkadhi' was absorbed day after day. With the time, his value and importance decrease between the residents.

The City of Algiers was indeed governed by 'Kara Hasan' who bears some ships anchored in the harbor but he couldn't go out to the Conquest as he hasn't sufficient number of sailors for that mission.

That way, after a period these ships if they are not maintained, they will be useless again and this will impact negatively on the City trading. It passed three years after our leave to Algiers, the number of delegations doubled asking us to return to the City. In meantime, 'Sinan Raiss' sailed in nine sea pieces for the Conquest, he captured twelve ships belonging to the kuffar then he advanced to Strait of 'Jabal Tarek' (Gibraltar in Spain mainland occupied now by UK) until he bombarded the south borders of Spain and rescued 800 Muslims fleeing the Spaniards oppression. They brought them all in his ships to Algeria.

I arranged to give them all the essentials, including lands, homes and money, to make them successful in their new life settlement. One day I saw 'Sinan Raiss' in a sad mood, I urged him: *"Sinan! What's going on? What do you have?* He replied:

*"What do you expect 'Basha', I can't no further be patient about what I'm looking, you and your brother Arruj Allah grant him the paradise, you gave huge efforts and sacrifices to seize Algiers, today we have the most magnificent harbor in North Africa in the hands of an Aarabi* (Bedouin) *guy who can't take advantage from it or allow us use it. Meanwhile, I'm coming back from Andalus* (Spain today), *it appears to me docking in Algiers harbor, he received me with Cannons shells. I could shut his Cannons and grabbing the entire city without pain, but I avoided your anger on me so I didn't. Now grant me approval to expel this dog called 'Ibn Alkadhi' and we settle in Algiers like we were before".*

# Chapter 27: Returning To The City

The delegations sent by Algerians never ceased, at the end, I invited 'Sinan Raiss' and I told him: "*Listen 'Raiss', it seems that the road to Algiers became paved for us, this Winter will be the last season that we spend in 'Jijel'. Inshallah, (if God wants) we will move to Algiers by the running of the Spring, 'Ibn Alkadhi' has not yet anyone who accepts him in the City. As you see there's not a single week passing without the coming of delegations begging us to return to Algiers, 'the excess of pampering bothers the lover', we must knock the iron as it's hot ", it's time for our return. For that I'll leave you here replacing and representing me in my family, ships and sailors. I'll come back to Algiers and when I'll enter it, I'll send to you what you should do*".

He answered me: "*Hearing and Obedience*". He stated that, and he went. I worked a lot during that Winter, I equipped my ships and I repaired my Cannons. The days passed quick, and we didn't notice until the Spring arrived adorned with flowers wreaths. And the delegations started again, coming from Algiers and other sectors. All of them were imploring me retiring to Algiers and administer it again. One of these delegations offered me a blonde mare the tongue can't describe her beauty. I accepted her with tremendous gratitude. I moved from ' Jijel' with 12000 sailors composed of 4000 Knights and 8000 Walkers and I didn't leave with 'Sinan Raiss' in 'Jijel' just

300 sailors. In the road, so many of the rural areas individuals joined us, all of them seeking entering Algiers with us. When we approached to the City, the guys of 'Ibn Alkadhi' attacked us. I bombarded them with bombs, to terrify him and then I ordered to fight them. 800 of them were murdered.

# Chapter 28: The End of "Ibn Alkadhi"

The blood of 'Ibn Alkadhi' was frozen when he knew us nearby to Algiers. He had 12000 Knights and 8000 Walkers, but he was doubtful about their desire or capacity to confront us. Even if they carry the weapons against us, they can't push us to not seize Algiers. Despite this, he tried to test his chance. One night, he attacked three military camps we placed on our way to Algiers. The result was he lose 185 men and 97 horses. Meanwhile, none was killed on our side. In the early morning, he re-attacked us again. His men were pretending to fight and most of them they escaped here and there to the mountains highs. This strange fight was durable until the evening where his Commander 'Kara Hasan' who was one of my sailors and rebelled against me, was killed. No other opportunity to 'Ibn Alkadhi' to survive. When he tried to slip away, one of Arabs Sheikh (Elders) stabbed him with a spear.

Then this Sheikh ordered to cut his head and delivered it to me. I offered the horse of 'Ibn Alkadhi' to this Sheikh with one hundred golden piece, this horse had an immense value, its price at least 1000 pieces of gold. When he was killed, the men of 'Ibn Alkadhi' throw their swords and get down on the ground as a sign of surrendering. The punishment of these miserable has no meaning, I pardoned and released them.

Meanwhile, some of them asked me to enter my service. I accepted. Those Arabs didn't experience obedience and Order, they never lived in a state that they belong to it. That way they were growing and that way they crossed their lives. In the same group, there were too some of my Turkish sailors coming from 'Alanadhool' (In Turkey) and served 'Ibn Alkadhi' with this treason they blackened the Turks faces.

After the perish of 'Ibn Alkadhi', they come to me standing up in my face, heads down, placing their hands over their chests expressing their surrendering as the Turks don't get down on ground like the Arabs.

Fast decision is one of my skills but I hesitated concerning my sailors. The origin of that is there are some of them who offered great services for us, thanks to them Spanish Commanders were killed and so many Spanish ships were captured too. Thousands of my sailors standing up in rows waiting for the verdict that I'll take toward their colleagues. The amnesty for these sailors was conditional, with many cares most critical one was its echo in Istanbul as they were considered rebellions against the Sultan 'Suleiman Khan' himself, as I represent him in Algeria.

Meanwhile, I think in what should I do, I felt a within voice insisting on me to pardon them. Abruptly I stated: "*I acquitted you all, pick up your weapons*". Their eyes welled up with tears, they took their weapons and they cannot raise out their heads from shame. I turned to their colleagues in rows. I saw in their eyes the sights of joy and recognition. It was assured for me later, the righteous of my decision as those sailors did all their efforts to erase the stain that pasted on them when they deceived me until the day when they killed all of them Allah grant them forgiveness.

# Chapter 29: Glorious Entry

After I dealt with the matters of 'Ibn Alkadhi' and other ones, we continued the walk and we arrived in Algiers City after one hour. The Elders were waiting in its entrance to receive us. When we entered the City, we went along its streets full of crowds applauding for us, expressing their enjoyment for our arrival. We hiked until we reached our old houses that we lived in before our leave. When I settled again, I tried my best to re-establish the stability and safety for the Capital and the citizens. At the same time, I assigned to 'Sinan Raiss' to bring my family and my ships to Algiers. He went out with 33 ships. When he reached the Algiers harbor, he sent shells into the air as a salutation from him. I responded in the same way from the Castle. This what occurred in Algiers.

For 'Telemsan,' the Sultan That I put him over its throne exploited my left of Algiers to repeal the mintage in the name of the greatest Sultan 'Suleiman Khan,' and print the coin with his own name. I wrote to him: "*You must print the money in the name of 'Khalifat Alzaman'* (Suleiman Alkanuni or the Magnificent) *and deliver the delayed taxes valued with 90000 dinars. The repeal of the mintage carrying the representative of the prophet Muhammad Peace and Blessings Be Upon him is an absolute crime. You should renew your faith immediately or I'll eliminate you from the earth as I did with 'Ibn Alkadhi'.*

When he got my letter, the king 'Abdallah' tore it. As a reaction to that, I backed his son 'Muhammad,' who revolted against his father requesting the 'Telemsan' throne. He took shelter in ridges with 2000 Knights. I prepared a troop and walked with to 'Telemsan', the prince 'Muhammad' pursued us in the road. He kissed my hand and joined my army. In meantime, the monarch 'Abdallah' moved out from 'Telemsan' and lead toward us. We met in 'Mazuna', where our forces clashed there. My army could disperse his forces and imprisoned him.

Immediately, I called for his head's cut. I wore his son the Sultanate's uniform and placed him on 'Telemsan' throne. I ordered 400 sailors to escort the new prince who sent later the requested taxes when he reached his city. The citizens of 'Telemsan' were very content with their new prince. In parallel to that, my sailors caught 'Farhat' the nephew of 'Ibn Alkadhi'. He calls for the amnesty as he hasn't any relationship with his uncle's revolution as he declared. He committed to pay 20000 dinars and he will be an efficient server for me. I made an agreement with him invoking that he never descend from the tribes mountains without my acceptance and he pay yearly 10000 dinars, one thousand Kamel, one thousand Cow, two thousands sheep, one hundred mules and twenty mares. When I returned to Algiers, I divided my fleet to small units, and I sent them to the Conquest under the command of 'Sinan Raiss'. On the night before the exit to the Conquest, I saw a wonderful 'Roaya' (religious concept of a dream as a message from God) drove me to perceive that she will be a blessed Conquest. Indeed, six of my ships returned carrying the same sum of kuffar ships.

One of them was shipped with gunpowder, lead and Cannon shells beside sixty bombs from the bronze. I was deeply happy with theses booties because we were in need for. The second ship was loaded with petroleum, tar, poles and Wood. The third one carried oils, olive oil, cheese and honey. The fourth with sugar and the last two were full of money. The first fleet returned to Algiers full of booties more than the other fleets. Best of all, nothing of my 35 ships were hurt. Thanks to Allah so much for his bounties.

The Spaniards had built a fortress on a rockets island called 'Ain Benian' (same name until now) stood three hundred meters from Algiers harbor. The fortress was guarded by hundreds of Spanish soldiers with hundreds of Cannons led by an aged old Captain named 'Don Martin Di Vargas' who was remarkable for a long time. The fortress was small. That's why the Spaniards couldn't put more soldier on it. The soldiers could not proceed to the shore. Even the drinking water that they have was coming from Balearic islands. In the past, the Spaniards were always destroying the harbor and its surroundings with bombs for that, the locals were obliged to answer their orders.

Now they stopped because of their fear of us, but we understood that allowing this grand rock in their hands is not a wise choice. I proposed to the Commander of the citadel "Don Vargas" to release it without battle and any damage to him and his soldiers. He rejected. As reply, I bombarded the fortress with shells along twenty days without giving up and after a tremendous battle, I got in her thus he and 700 of his guys surrendered.

# Chapter 30: A Spaniard In A Cannon

When the fortress was in the hands of the Spaniards, they were bombing the minarets of the mosques in the time of the prayers calling (Adane) They did this just for amusement. But when we settled in Algiers, they stopped this heinous behavior worrying us. Thus, made them unhappy. When we took up this fortress, it came to me the detained artillery commander who was the first responsible for the minarets' destruction and for the assassination of several 'Adane callers'. I told him: *"Oh infidel, you are an excellent sniper. You ruin any minaret with a single shell. Look now how it will be the true sniping"*.

Then, I ordered to place him in a cannon mouth and throw him into the sea. Also, I beat the neck of his assistant and ten of his artillery soldiers. I put the rest in the jail. We didn't have any need for this citadel. I mined and detonated it. After that, I gathered 30 000 infidel prisoners in Algeria; I decided to use them in construction of a Waves broker connecting the fortress with the harbor using its rocks. That way, we could be made a magnificent and secure harbor for Algiers city. My seizing of the castle makes Carlos, the Spain king, frantic even as he cut the head of the emissary who notified him.

He announced: "*The confiscation of the garrisons is the working of the glorious emperors like me. How a sea thief like Barbarossa dared to pick up my castle? In the time when I conquered the France king and putting him in one of Madrid dungeons, I couldn't push a pirate like this? Surely, the original cause for that returns to the incapability of my commanders in land and sea. You place my face on soil, go out now.*" It was one of my habits to invite the kuffar commanders, captains, priests, artists, governors, who fell hostages, to talk with them and argue about various matters.

I didn't ask them shortly to extract the information from them, but I was communicating with them as a friend perform. With that strategy, I gained from them precious clue. Even I was always aware of the vital secrets unknown in Europe palaces. The truth that I should mention here that I have spies in the entire Mediterranean countries. But sitting with the prisoners of war and dialoguing with them is better to gain the information. What Carlos said after I grabbed the rocky fortress came to me with that way. I knew too from one of captives that Carlos is now in Barcelona and he traveled to Genoa, which is like so many European kingdoms' belongings to Carlos.

His highest Admiral called 'Andrea Doria' was too from Genoa. After the destruction of the Spanish castle, a flotilla of ships unaware of that, came with the supplies to the soldiers. They didn't find the castle they thought they missed the road they continued the sailing until they find themselves surrounded by 15 ships of ours in front of the Algerians eyes.

We overcome most of them meanwhile 350 surrendered sent to prison. This incident left behind an attitude that the

Spanish ships could not yet approach the Algerian coasts. In the meantime, my highest commander 'Sinan Raiss' collapsed in ill health. I forwarded the commandment to' Idin Raiss.''Idin', who was more expert in sea work and more courageous than 'Sinan Raiss'. In a day, I invited him and I explained him: *"my son 'Idin' you'll leave out this year for the conquest in the west of the Mediterranean sea.You should sail until you enter the Cebta (Ceuta) strait. When you come back occupy the Spain coasts without making them getting you. Then take with you the biggest numbers as you can from our brothers the Muslims refugees in Granada mountains. Take them all to Algiers. My blessed supplication will be with you but don't forget to look at the necessary to succeed in this mission"*. He replied: *"On the head and eye Basha"*. He goodbye me and quit.

He selected ten ships and applied my plans until he crossed five enormous 'kaderga' model ships. He began a great battle with her sailors. He defeated them all, seized the ships and sent her to Algiers with Turkish men. In the day eleven, from his left of the harbor, these five ships were docked. I was glad about that because they were military ships with an exceptional quality. In other hand, 'Idin Raiss' still sweeping on the Spanish cities on the south coast, bombarding them with shells and detaining the Spaniards. He rescue too the escaping Muslims that he encountered until his ships were entirely full. When he heard that 'Idin Raiss' transported thousands of Muslims, the Spanish king Carlos ordered one of his great admirals named 'Portondo' to cut his returning road and he promised him a 10 000 golden piece prize if he accomplish this mission.

With a huge fleet 'Portondo' faced 'Idin' ships who discussed with 'Salah Rais' one of his sea captains in how to push this attack. They were convinced that if they prefer to manage adequately the battle, they should descend the Andalucian immigrants on the beach. When they'll finish with the Spaniards, they'll return and took them to Algiers. When they realized this decision, the Andalucians entered into a state of melancholy and fear. They cried and refused to descend. Most of them were children and women.'Idin' and 'Salah' Raiss were obliged to force them leaving the ships.

Their presence in the ships reflects a major risk and a handicap for the sailors on the stage of fighting with the Spaniards. The Spanish ships approached gravely. Idin and Salah did a brutal fast attack, clashed with them in a harsh fight ended by the seizing of seven enormous Spanish ships, 'Portondo' who enslaved and tortured thousands of Spain Muslims families, was killed.

Also, his entire commanders and captains were killed. 'Idin Raiss' won this battle thanks to the cooperation of 'Salah Rais' who was well known about his malinity and smart. Even he was described as he can make the fox leave his home thanks to his intelligence!

From the date of this battle, the christians named the Turks as 'The Satan and Infidel Beater'. Beside the massive ships, 350 Spaniards were apprehended, the rest were killed. Muslim prisoners tied to the paddles were too detached.

For the Andalucian immigrants, they were watching the battle from the beach. After its end, they were brought again to the ships and transported to Algiers. In the meantime, 'Sinan Raiss' died. After a while, I invited ' Idin Raiss'. He entered and kissed my hand. I nominated him as the commander of the fleet in the place of the blessed departed 'Sinan Raiss and

I nominated too 'Salah Rais' as second commander.'I projected to send 'Idin Raiss' to Istanbul as he was a captain on some units of the ottoman fleet when he was there.

The sultan 'Biazid Althani', Allah give him mercy, assigned him to Egypt to serve the 'Almamluki' sultan there. He came from there to Algiers and remained with my brother 'Arruj Raiss'. Before sending him to Istanbul, I prepared three ' kaderga' ships and prepared them with all the necessary. I decorated too the poles with Genoa gold until she appeared from a distance brilliant with the sunshine. Truly, she was incredibly beautiful. Even the dialect can't describe it. Also, I put in each one 100 sailor and I choose for her the strongest rowers. Besides all this, I distinguished 300 prisoners who will be sent as a gift to the king of land and sea 'Suleiman Khan'. When everything was fixed, the sailors comes to me and kissed my hand, then they leave Algiers under the tones of cannon shells.

# Chapter 31: Welcome "Idin Raiss"

In a blessed hour, Idin Raiss entered Istanbul under the salutation of the cannon's shells. When the ships anchored, the 300 prisoners descended with wonderful clothes. Each one of them carries specific types of spoils. Meanwhile, the inhabitants flooded from everywhere to regard the Algerian fleet. It was a grand honor to Idin Raiss and other sailors to meet his greatness 'Suleiman Khan' and pass to him the letter that I sent. With humbles, he read it by himself. When he finished, he thanked Idin Raiss and honored him. At the end of the meeting, he ordered for him as a prize 400 dinars and 300 for his accompanied sailor. He also gave 100 dinars to nine of my captains and the same amount for the ships Imams (like the priests in Christianity). Also 50 dinars for every military captain. He offered too to Idin Raiss a studded sword, a Sultabate's dress and a military telescope.

For the sailors, he ordered to receive them in the 'guests house' beside the factory of the ship's construction where they enjoyed themselves during their residence. The sultan gave his new orders for 'Idin Raiss' who later visited the ministers and the directors. He stayed a complete month in Istanbul. At the end of his visit, he met again the sultan, who gave him a studded sword and knife, a suit studded with gold and a flag tailored too with gold and two medals decorated with diamonds, he addressed him to bring them to me.

Beside this, he instructed three 'kaderga' model ships with twenty paddles each one. He furnished her with newly fabricated bombs. Its stock stores were charged with the varied military equipment, including oil, tar, thick ropes, sails, poles and diverse other things. The ship was absolutely full with anything that we would lack it. The materials were heavy until the entire fleet could sink in water. When 'Idin Raiss' preparing himself to leave, the sultan called him again and offered him a medal studded with diamonds, something to make him intensely glad and content.

The sultan descended to his coastal Palace to watch my fleet leaving. My ships saluted him with bombs in the air, continuing their line to Mediterranean, then to Algiers. 'Idin Raiss' passed in front of 'Olenia' coasts after 'darash' ones until he entered Venice gulf. After a while there, he left running through Sicily, then 'Balears' islands. He invaded her and seized booties and a considerable number of hostages from 'Mallorca' island.

Later, he returned to Algiers. 'Idin Raiss' left Algiers with ten 'kaderga' model ships and returned with three ships with same model beside fifteen smaller ones. He seized her in his come back way. His fleet transformed to 25 pieces! We were truly satisfying when we saw him entering Algiers harbor. We find his ship's booties loaded with huge quantities of coffee, rice, silk cloth, mirrors, guns and shooters. I received him and he handed me the letter of his majesty packed with a silk paper.

I took her, kissed her three times, and put her over my head. Then I opened it and find written: " *'Beylar Bey' of*

*Algiers, your message is already coming to us, we realize and appreciate your interesting performances. The 300 prisoners are received and I ask Allah to support you and your companions and whiten your faces in this life and afterlife. I sent to you the military equipment to push up our enemy, the infidel Spaniards. Put the medal in your turban and my flag on your ships. For my white flag fabricated with gold put it in a position showing your dignity and should never fall on ground".*

I placed the sultan flag in a high position in the big door of Algiers. Daily, we salute it under ottoman military music twice, one in the morning by rising it and the second in the evening by descending it. And when we go out to the conquest, I placed it on highest point of the ship sail. In a year, I gathered the poor orphans, boys and girls. I did the circumcision for the little boys and married the girls who reached the marriage age. I gave each one his lack of money. I ordered too to deliver houses for whose without shelter and give them jobs. I was confident that Allah gave back to us times more than we spent on the poor. I saw this and lived it along my life. Every time I spent something from my fortune, fastly, Allah give back to me tens of times.

# Chapter 32: The Kings Mockery

You make me a Mockery Between the Kings, no one of you can defeat Barbarossa. All what's occurred at this meeting arrived to me with details and in the fastest way. My spies infiltrated in Europe told me about all that. The spies acting for the Christians were dispersed too in Algeria. Them too, they afford them with all the crucial information about me and my men.

To avoid the leaks of the secret information from Algeria, I was behaving in a natural manner. But it was impossible to stop the news about our military movements, especially the Algiers harbor considered one of the biggest harbors in trading and volume of ships. Andrea Dorea goes out with the hope that he catches me. The king Carlos put on his disposal twenty Spanish ships and ten venetian ships, all from the model 'kaderga'. These ships were clearly bigger than ours that we use. At the same time, ours are more fast and easy to maneuver than theirs. In the meantime, I have already 35 ships with the same model 'kaderga'. I placed on her the sailors 'Kurd oglo', 'Mosleheddine Raiss' and directed them to be ready for the future battle. I was informed about the entrance of 'Andrea Doria' to Mallorca island coming from other Balearic isles.

Despite his commitment to his emperor to arrest me, he didn't dare to invade Algiers harbor. Instead, he bombed

'Harshal' harbor, which had been guarded by several hundreds of sailors. When they saw his fleet approaching 'Harshal', they took refuge in the fortress by blocking her gates. Meanwhile, his men were robbing and kidnapping everything and everyone in the city. The sailors took advantage of this opportunity, they opened the doors and attacked 'Daria' men. This was extremely surprising Dorea, as he thought that fear was behind their refuge to the castle. The sailors set their swords on the enemy's necks, who were dissipated on the city roads looking for spoils and not expecting a fight. So many of them were murdered as a consequence the others run away to their ships. Meantime 1700 were detained. At the moment of being aware of his attack on 'Harshal', I went out to 'Dorea' with 40 sea pieces. But he escaped from me when he heard about my approaching to fight him.

I found a flotilla left in tail I clashed with them and I seized the ships after a hard fight. When the fight was on his extreme, the Muslim prisoners on the Spanish ships broke their chains screaming' Ya Allah' (calling for God's help).The battle finished with the martyrdom of 300 of us and our confiscation of the fleet. The number of my ships became 60, including the ones of the enemy. I brought them all to 'Harshal' harbor. Seven ships of my fleet were brought by 'Sinan Raiss' from Djerba island.

In the meantime, I counted the number of Muslim prisoners that I liberated from them. I found them at 2700. I gave them their choice to choose their future destination. Some of them prefer to work for me and others I offered them the necessary money supporting them returning to their homelands. For the total of infidel prisoners, they were 1900, including one with the grade of an admiral. It was too a great commander. I ordered to attach all of them to the paddles to work on rowing. For me, I stayed just for hours in 'Harshal' then I left for Algiers which I reach three days after leaving her.

# Chapter 33: The Atlantic Ocean

I wanted to capture 'Andrea Doria'. For that purpose, I placed 'Idin' over a big fleet and directed him to pursue him. He sailed until Ceuta, proceeding to the enemy coasts until he reached Gibraltar. From there to the Atlantic ocean but he didn't cross anyone. Thus, he decided to retire to Algiers. In his course, he bombarded Balearic and Minorca islands and the coasts of the Mediterranean sea. By these tremendous attacks, he could imprison 3000 kaffer. He even approached the Barcelona harbor. It was a great monastery near to this harbor was yearly, visited by Spanish princes and kings. 'Idin Raiss' invaded it. He detained 80 priests and seized 36 boxes from the warehouses.

The chandlery that he seized present 25 keyl of silver. This attack was a strong slap for the king Carlos' arrogance putting his face on ground. The number of captivated ships in this conquest was 55 ships between big and small ones. He retired them all to Algiers. With this succeeded invasion, we give the good answer to 'Andrea Doria' attack on Harshal. As a consequence, the Algiers markets became very cheap in comparison to Indian ones. The merchants were buying with one dirham and sell with ten something that makes them very rich! The number of prisoners rise to 16 000 without the ones working on rowing and those who works on houses. From these prisoners, I choose 500 best ones to send them to Istanbul to work as rowers. I gave this mission to 'Idin Raiss', who took them all with 15 'kaderga' model ships.

On the day 27 after his left of Algiers, he entered Istanbul, and he delivered my letter to the world sultan 'Suleiman Khan' who generously read it by himself. He visited too all the ministers and the state departments and deliver them too the gifts that I sent to them. He got deep respect and honor from them.

Later, the sultan 'Suleiman Khan' appealed to him again and told him: "*Listen Raiss, I inform you that all the acquires that obtained 'Algiers 'Beylar Bey' kaireddine Barbarous have a deep respect for me. That's why I'll give you now five 'kaderga' model ships you deliver them for him. I ordered too 'Kobtan Basha' to give you all the necessary bombs, shells and the military equipment that you need, especially the sea cannons shells, take from them as much as you want. And I'll send with you a number of 'cannons engineers' to be under your service. Our fleet in Algiers must be the strongest possible and be ready for the fight at any time. It came to me that the king Carlos has a bad intention to Algiers. Be careful and take the needed precautions*".

Idin Raiss arrived at Algiers in the day 41 after his left of Istanbul. He left with 15 'kaderga' ships. Five of them were a gift offered by the sultan 'Suleiman Khan. In his way, he seized seven other ships that he used in attacking infidel cities and captivating 700 from them. Idin Raiss gave me the sultan letter stamped with the white ottoman stamp. I kissed the box containing the letter three times, and I put it over my head, expressing my glorifying for the sultan. Then I took the letter from the box, read it carefully until I retained all the sultan's orders. After I took the gifts offered for me by the sultan, which were a sultanate suit fabricated from the precious fur, a golden watch and a studded sword beside the ottoman flag.

In the meantime, the king Carlos was preoccupied with other things, his brother the king of Vienna Fernando asked him support. At the same time, the sultan 'Suleiman Khan' confirming on his captains on the hungarian borders to not give any breath for Fernando when invading his kingdom. Carlos recognized that he can't defeat us, so he pressed the 'Telemsan' king to revolute against us. He furnished him with colossal amounts of money. And as this sultan too saw that he's the legitimate sultan, he too, he shared his promises to his surroundings if they support him.

Carlos, after his long experience of invading and governing, recognized too that the main way to defeat any enemy in case of his failure in invasion, he supports the greed in the rule. The sultan of Telemsan believed Carlos' promises, and he declared his revolution against us. Thus, I ordered 'Delly Mehmet Raiss' to exit to the conquest in the sea.

For me, I took my men and went to Telemsan that was near to 'Fass' city. I found just a little resistance that pushed the Telemsan sultan to flee. Then he sent to me the savants to demand the amnesty. I said to them: *"I'll forgive him when he Will come by himself apologizing"*. Later, he came to me and he pays me the delayed taxes with 111 000 dinars. Then he sit on his knees and touched my foot.

I told him: *"Leave that, infidel, and restore your faith. You helped our great enemy against me and you know that I represent the Caliphate of the Muslims, the world sultan. You set your sword in my face"*

He declared his repentance, he said 'Shahadatain' and he repeated his joining to Islam and he renew his marriage to his wives. When I was in Telemsan, 'Delly Mehmet' crossed in the sea with his 40 ships fleet, a Spanish one with 35 ships. Fastly they clashed together. After a violent fight, 29 ships captured. Meanwhile, the other six ran away. When this news reached the Spanish king residing in Barcelona, he was at the point of dying. Furthermore, he can't even speak with a single word, especially after his failure against the world sultan 'Suleiman Khan' in Germany.

# Chapter 34: The Campaign To Spain

When my triumphs reached the Andalucian Muslims, they became more courageous, and they claimed the revolution. Thus 80 000 from who were residing in mountains fearing the Spaniards descended to the cities and attacked this enemy. They put on them so many defeats. At the moment when I knew about these revolutions, I ordered 'Mehmet Raiss' with a fleet of 36 ships to support the rebels with their needs. Until this date, I did 21 campaigns in the coastal Spanish cities. Each time, we bring thousands of Muslims, including women, kids, olds and youths, saving them from the torture and burning of the Spaniards to the north Africa cities. I was the header of the fleet in the majority of these campaigns. The same did 'Sinan Raiss' and 'Idin Raiss' on so many occasions. Allah gives them good and mercy for their jihad. The infidels of Spain don't resemble for the other European ones.

They were in an outrageous tyranny and arrogance. Eager for the bloods like the raged dogs. The sultan 'Suleiman Khan' was like his father Salim Khan and his grandfather 'Biazid Khan' never missed the help of Andalus Muslims. Allah gave them the paradise. As his great interest to the Muslims there, I received from him in several occasions letters dealing with this matter. One day, a messenger comes to Algiers named 'Sinan Agha' assigned by his greatness. He presented to me a letter. I took her, kissed her three times and putting her over my head, showing my deep respect and honor for his sender. I opened it and I read: *"To the 'Beylar Bey' of the Arabic state (Iyala) of Algeria, the conqueror' Khaireddine Basha', be notified that I have the intention to conquer the king of Spain. When this letter reaches you, put a trusty man for you in our place. In case you can't find someone, inform me about that"*.

Instantly after I finish the reading, I told 'Sinan Agha', this is the conduct of our master, I'll go fastly to Istanbul to be honored to meet him to see what he desire. Without wasting time, I started preparing for the travel.When this information arrived to Carlos, he was horrified and he ordered his first admiral Andrea Dorea to cut my way and prohibit me to attains Istanbul.

The situation required that I exited to Istanbul with a great fleet as I foresaw an attack from the Spaniards. In other view; I was convinced that if I leave Algeria with a limited number of guards, the thousands of prisoners will revolute and this will create so much trouble.To forbid that, I invited my relative 'Mahmoud Raiss' who was the responsible for supervising these prisoners. And I give him a direct order to open his eyes on their behaviors. We open the sails and we leave Algiers in a blessed hour.

I had 26 'kaderga' ships with me. Meanwhile, I left the other pieces in Algiers and in the west of the Mediterranean. And by the help of Allah, I could capture in my way 18 other infidel ships. Our destiny was that we entered Istanbul with 44 ships. I was accompanied on this travel by 18 captains of the sea. All of them were prominent in the Mediterranean. We couldn't pass near the south Italian coasts belonging to Spain without bombing or invading her. Our master, the sultan, was in an open war with Spain.

For that, we raided on the western beaches of Sardinia island. Then we move to the north until we reached Genoa zones. From there, I sailed sided to the Italian coasts until I arrived at 'Macina' harbor, where I found a Spanish fleet formed by 18 pieces. I seized her all. I attached her to my ships and retired her after a dangerous battle in the sea large. With this conquest, my dream became true by entering the happiness to the sultan's heart, who aimed overcoming Spain. For the 'Andrea Doria', who considered himself the greatest infidel captain, was at these events, sailing on 'Almora' beaches.

When he was informed about my success in 'Macina', he became terrified. He ran away to the 'ionic' archipalgo. I pursued him there but I couldn't catch and detaining him and I don't know where does he concealed. After a while, I knew he hide in Genoa. I sent 25 ships to search for 'Dorea'. They coincide with a 'Dorea' flotilla formed by seven pieces. Two of them surrendered after clashes. Meanwhile, five escaped. For me, I left the ionic islands directed to the south until 'Almora' coasts.

At this time' Ahmad Basha' a 'Daria captain' anchoring with a part of the ottoman fleet in 'Navarone' harbor in the southwest of 'Almora' island. When we saw each other, we bombed shells in the air, saluting each other. I met him and we decided then to sail to Istanbul. We reached it on a sunny day of the winter. Despite the cold, Istanbul inhabitants come out of their homes to welcome us. Their number was nearing 200 000 people. It passed hours and we send our shells to the sky, saluting our grand sultan and the City which holds the world throne and for Istanbul inhabitants, known for their knowledge, honor and kindness. We rode a boat with 18 famous sea captains. Beside several sailors accompanying me in a best dress.

I saluted the citizens who received us with great and true love, expressing it with continuous applauding.200 prisoners heading the carnival. Each one carries the most splendid sculptures in Europe manufactured by gold and silver. Following them 30 from the nobles of Europe, all of them were admirals and captains even between them, relatives to the king Carlos. Following these also 200 slaves bringing over their arms bags full of gold and silver. Then 200 boys bringing in their necks diamonds, each one has rolls of cloth and silk tailored with gold and silver.

Behind them 200 beautiful odalisques following the carnival. They wore wonderful clothes from the top quality silk, displaying expensive diamonds. After all that, passed 100 livestock charged with booties. Followed by rare animals brought from Africa like panthers, giraffes, lions and others leaded by a number of trainers. For me, sea captains and some sailors, we were walking behind wearing simple clothes until the palace of 'Topkape Sarayee'. I was extremely happy when I arrived at the palace that handles the world. And as I saw and heard, Istanbul inhabitants never saw a carnival like ours in its elegance, cost, and curiosity. For the truth, only Allah knows it. In the next day, we were invited me and 18 from the sea captains to meet the sultan 'Suleiman Khan'. When we entered to him, each one kissed his hand and he, he thanks us and described us with the best words ever given to anyone before.

# Chapter 35: "Daria Captain" Title

The welcome of the sultan for us was tremendously honorable and impressive. The members of the sultanate council assembled for a specific meeting. Presented on it all the ministers whose took place in two rows siding the grand sultan. The only missed minister was the 'great chest' (prime minister) 'Makbul Basha' who was in 'Halab' (Syrian city, same name until today). He left Istanbul for 68 days to Iran conquest. Will all his modesty, the sultan accepted the gifts that I offered for him.

He recompensed me and the sailors' headers with me by ordering for us each one a sultanate dress. I don't remember in my entire life the happiness that I enjoyed as what I felt when the sultan honored and prized us. Through the assembly, he addressed me with a speech: *"Listen 'Basha' I want to make you 'Daria Captain' to command our sultanate fleet in your conquering wars. You should know too that I'll not take the Algeria state from you, but I'll place you on it as a ' Beylar Bey'. But you should choose a good person to represent you there and he must be a responsible managing her in your name. To be suitable to manage those two titles, you should meet the great chest settling now in 'Halab'. Hurry, ride your horse and meet him. When you'll return, we will talk again"*. After the end of the council, the sultan talked with me privately and he informed me that he wants to occupy Spain.When he mentioned Andrea Dorea, I couldn't control myself and I said: *"Mawlay*(my master), *this dog called Andrea Dorea don't merit that your blessed lips talk about him"*.

Then I realized that I made a mistake by talking in such manner in his highness presence. I became ashamed of reacting like that. The sultan Suleiman Khan was very polite even he saw my reaction, smiled and pointed with his hand, signaling that there's no problem with talking like that. I was relaxed. When my meeting concluded, I left the council after his permission.

I resided several days in Istanbul before I took a rapid horse path to Halab, which I reach after ten days of continuous run. Based on what is spoken; it was never a case that anyone before me crossed the distance between Istanbul and Halab in this short period. In this travel, I spent a night in 'Bursa' and other in 'Konia'. Except those two nights, when I felt exhausted, I descend from my horse and sleep for two hours, then continue my voyage.

When I reached 'Konia' city, I visited the tomb of 'Malwana' 'Jalal Aldine Alrumi'. In the day ten, I entered Halab palace where the grand minister' Ibrahim Pasha' lodge. He was in the forties of his age, the same age as our sultan. Kind and smart. I stayed two days through them, we discussed the political circumstances in Europe and the conquests done by the 'himayun' (sultanate) fleet. When we finished, he declared my nomination as 'Daria Captain', wore me the sultanate suit then he goodbye me. I reached Istanbul after the same ten days. I was deeply happy to command the greatest fleet in the entire world. The fleet that makes all the European fleets together incapable to defeat it.

# Chapter 36: Admiral Of Ottoman Fleet

I hurried up to the house of the ship's construction in Istanbul. It were several ships factories spread across different cities. But the greatest one was in the gulf of the gold horn. This factory was incomparable worldwide from the side of his capacity of holding a considerable number of ships, the number of workers and the number of specialities and professionals.

The workers and apprentices were in majority from the Christians. For the engineers and the technicians, all of them were Turks. The Christian workers didn't work for free. They were paid each time they finish their tasks. Thus, so many of them request their freedom and they return to their home countries. The number of workers was not less than 20 000 workers. In case of need, we could construct a fleet equivalent to the Venice empire one just in a single year. In reality, the name of Istanbul's factory reached the horizons. Even some of the Venetians in the periods of peace, they requested from the sultan Suleiman Khan that he accepts some of their ships be maintained in this factory.

I wasn't able to identify the volume of the ottoman fleet before I see it by myself. With such factory and the assistance of our sultan and before all this, by the support of Allah, we could achieve what we desire. I suggested to 'Ibrahim Pasha', the prime minister to target campaigns to the new world (America continents) newly discovered. We will benefit a lot. But he didn't permit us, sufficient for him that we maintain control over the Mediterranean and the Indian ocean. In the time when I was the manager in the ship's factory and the built of new boats, I was discovering Istanbul areas.

I visited all the tombs of ottoman sultans and I read for them Surat Alfatiha (chapter of The opening in Quran). Also, I helped all what I met whose in need in my way. I realized there that our fame is already expanded. I found the all there, knows me and knows about all our sea battles. The Istanbul inhabitants were loving us and respect us profoundly. I was feeling the same for them. Through my life, I visited a huge number of counties and kingdoms, just a few left. I didn't visit. But on this visit, I never seen a beauty like the elegance of Istanbul strait. each angle of it is like a part of the paradise. I'll buy a land part in the strait beside Marmara sea, I'll make it my tomb when I'll die Inshallah (if God wants).

My nomination over the Ottoman Empire fleet made reactions in the European capitals. Especially the king Carlos, who felt a great danger from this step. When the spring settle, I went out with 80 ships from the ottoman fleet. Until I reached 'Macina' strait. The Macina harbors were located on Sicily island coasts neighboring Italian Rogeo. I seized all of them and I carried 16 000 prisoners in my ships.

In this campaign, I occupied 18 castles. I sent their keys with 16000 prisoners and 425 giant booties boxes on 40 'kaderga' ships to Istanbul. The other 40 ships stayed for me for a while. Both the great sultan and the prime minister were satisfied about my management for the fleet and the conquests that I did in sea large. But some of the envy men of the state who weren't hesitant to talk about me. They discussed between them: "*Look at what he does our master, the sultan. He nominated a pirate over the Ottoman Empire with the degree of an admiral!*"

Those envy persons who talked like that, never conquered a single fortress in his life. Never seizing a single enemy ship. But my sultan never leave an opportunity to honor me and talk positively about me and my accomplishments. His respect was accumulating with the flow of days. When they saw this, they locked their mouths from talking. They can no longer express their mad feelings after the slap of his majesty on their faces. My second destination with the 'Admiral' title was to Sardinia island.

From there to Algiers, then Tunis which its sultan left her, frightened and seek safety in the desert. I entered Tunis, then I invaded so many cities to the south until Kairouan city. Later I come back to Tunis again.The sultan of Tunis was a member of 'Hafssiun' dynasty who extended her domination over North Africa in a day. He couldn't delay his calling for help from the king Carlos to regain his throne.This last one accepted, and he committed to come to Tunis to eliminate us. Thus, I arranged myself to fight him. In that winter, I sent my ships to the west of the Mediterranean sea on Spanish coasts.

For the fleet that I moved to Sardinia, he returns with 12 000 pieces of gold, 475 prisoners beside other booties. At the end, the emperor Carlos himself was over an armada in Tunis coasts. The fleet was carrying thousands of soldiers gathered from the kingdoms subject to Carlos like France, Italy,

Belgium, Netherlands and other ones. He reached Tunis, after 17 days of his left of Barcelona, in 500 ships, some for military use and others for soldiers' transportation.. The conquest of Tunis requires the seizing of Halk Alwadi castle. To forbid the Spaniards doing this, I instructed Ikhane Raiss, who was one of best sailors headers, to guard it. The Spaniards besieged the castle. Carlos himself lead his infidel army.

Ikhane Raiss has 120 cannons, and the enemy has hundreds of cannons on land and sea. He attacked the enemy three speed times, killing 6000 infidel soldiers. For me I was waiting for the reaction of Tunis sultan, 'Mawlay Alhasan' who ran to desert. I had 11000 soldiers but half of them were from the volunteers bedouins who ignores the war basics. And never minded running away when the fight became harder.

All what I wanted was to fight as long as I can in Halk Alwadi. Fastly, I issued my orders to move fastly the ottoman fleet to Tunis. If the fleet arrived in the due time, Carlos will find himself between two hells and he will be defeated. Carlos was aware of that, too. That's why he was eager to occupy Halk Alwadi and never caring about his losses. In one of campaigns led by 'Ikhan Raiss', he could kill two of best Spaniards army captains who were 'Sarno' and 'Mondea' princess. For the 'Mawlay Alhasan', he was on his way to us with 1600 knights and 8000 camel loaded with food and the war needs.

When it became clear that the fall of halk Alwadi is a matter of time, the revolution symptoms started too to emerge. the 6000 volunteers bedouins who seek for Carlos satisfaction, started to revolute. I didn't find any available solution just to direct to the south. Their treason manifested when they opened the prison doors to liberate 10 000 infidel prisoners.

Surely there are whom between these bedouins who have sympathy with Turks and are loyal to their religion.

But the misinformation spread by Tunis sultan and his spies about the coming of Spaniards to liberate them from Turks and never they'll put their swords on Muslims, push them to do this offensive action. We found ourselves between two blades, from a side we should fight 10 000 infidels controlling the city in other side, we should fight against the real enemy, the Spanish army. This situation made our standing up impossible. Meanwhile, Halk Alwadi fell, but 'Ikhan Raiss' could retire with some Turks and join us.

He merits a great respect especially, after I thought that he'll never survive. His efficient skills helped him to escape the coil made by the surrounding enemy. Despite all this, I resisted in Tunis for six another days after the fall of Halk Alwadi and I generated from the Spaniards' expensive losses. By joining us by 'Ikhan', my army raised to 9700 soldiers. But in the presence of 30 000 Spanish soldiers, 500 ships in north and the Mawlay Alhasan forces in the south, defeating them became an impossible matter.

Furthermore, 40 cannons with ammunition were captured by them in Halk Alwadi. Mawlay Alhasan goes to the Spanish camp and kissed Carlos' feet. And thanks to him, he gathered more Arabs to fight us. In my first clash with both forces together, I lost 2500 martyrs. The war calculations show that I can't push them with the rest of 7200 soldiers. We were in summer time, the temperature is in high. I concluded the last raid on the enemy. When I wanted to retire to the city. I was surprised by the closing of the city doors by the inhabitants.

Initially, it was a newly Muslim person called Jaafar who opened the prisons doors for the kuffar. I made a huge attack to disperse the enemy. The voices of sailors screaming: Allah, Allah, make the enemy hearts horrified. In this battle, thousands of martyrs fell . Most of them were from Marash areas. Allah only knows how I wished to be a martyr like them. I would be happy for my survival, but thinking about the Europe kings who participated in this campaign just to kill me or see me imprisoned in chains makes me persistent to fight until the end.

I thank Allah for protecting me and I'll never leave the martyrs blood goes for free. Few of injured sailors beside 'Idin Raiss 'and 'Ikhan Raiss' were the only who stayed with me. I crossed Tunis gulf from extreme to extreme until I reached 'Anaba' city confronting the southwest of Sicily island where 14 'kaderga' ships were waiting for us. In the meantime, Idin Raiss' sinks into the sea and died a martyr. I ask Allah to place him in a prominent position in a paradise, he and all other sailors who fight against the Europeans. And over them all 'Kamal Raiss, who was the teacher of my brother.

# Chapter 37: Tunis Massacre

Tunis was one of greatest African cities. When they invaded it, they killed 30 000 Arabic Muslims and enslaved 10 000 women and Childs, destroying the mosques, the schools and the tombs and they rob the castles too. They burned also thousands of books and scientific papers located in libraries. That way, they erased several kinds of sciences and arts. When the infidels realized that I escaped from their hands; they put their angry on the innocent inhabitants. They were loyal to their satanic souls.

After 72 hours of the campaign of killing, stealing and devastating, Carlos entered to the city after he transformed it into remains. His horse's legs stained with the blood of the innocents debris spread on the roads and corners of the city. That way, the city of Tunis and its neighborhood fell. And the 'Hafsits' surrendered to the Spaniards. Meanwhile, the southern and eastern regions remained under our control. For Tunis, it was under our administration just for eleven months. I arrived at Algiers' camping from Tunis.

Then I went out with 32 sea pieces until I reached the Balearic islands. I bombed the 'Minorca' and Mallorca' islands. I captivated 5500 individuals from 'Mahone' and 'Palma' harbors. After that, I continued to the Atlantic ocean via Ceuta strait and I sailed with my fleet in 'Khadiz' gulf located between Spain and Portugal. Where I destroyed 'Faro' harbor south of Portugal.

And I seized a huge ship equipped with 76 cannons carrying 300 sailors and push her hundreds of rowers. She was coming from India loaded with precious Indian merchandises. Besides 36 000 golden dinars. The beauty of the ship and its luxuriousness forbidden me to go down it.

Thus, I retired her to Algiers. After a while, I traveled to Istanbul, and I was received by his highness, my sultan, in his private council where I informed him about all the events occurred and especially in Tunisian lands. His majesty was pleased to accept my gifts that were a rosary fabricated with pearls, a ring with diamonds and golden watch and three rare birds. The value of these gifts was 12 000 Akja. Later, I visited the ministers and delivered them my gifts. I paid the one fifth from the spoils to the state Treasury. After I finished my official visits, I went to the ship's factory. I sit in my office and I asked about the information and events when I was outside Turkey.

Then I invited the engineers header and ordered him to start building 30 'kaderga' ships. Because I was near to exit to the conquest with our master, the sultan! After our preparation for this, I commanded a fleet. Meanwhile, my sultan went on land over an army until the 'Adriatic' sea. My campaign targeted the kingdoms of Venice and Spain as my sultan wants to occupy the harbor of 'Otarento' in southern Italy. After conquering Venice and island of 'Korfo' beside Spain, I entered 'Adriatic' sea, I saw a venetian ship, I ordered to seize her. Then we sank 14 pieces of ' kaderga' and we captured too other 16 ships. Meantime, other fleet pieces ran away.

The ' Beylar Beys', the ministers and the officials come to the commanding ship and congratulates us for this great .conquest. Later, my sultan returned to Istanbul by land and me I returned with the fleet.The next year, I went out to' Ija' sea, meanwhile my sultan went via land to conquest the 'Boligdan'.

This time, the kuffar has not any existence in 'Ija' except in islands of 'Kerba' and 'Kashut' which I was near to invade. I was near too to burn 'Crit' island coasts and oblige the Venetians to sign a mutual compromise. But an anticipation of an attack from 'Andrea Doria' to 'Salah Raiss', who is coming in his way from Alexandria, pressed me to issue orders going there to protect his flotilla as a primordiality. 'Salah Raiss carried the India treasures sent by the 'Bahadur Shah' of ' Gujarat' who was one of greatest India kings.

Who request from us to help him to eliminate the Portuguese from India that's why, after six days of my leaving Istanbul and 25 days before the leave of my sultan to the jihad, Beylar Bey of Egypt called 'Suleiman Basha' left 'Suez' harbor with a great fleet to the Indian ocean there's no one hated by 'Andrea Doria' on earth after me like 'Salah Raiss'. This brave and intelligent man makes the emperors, admirals and captains of Europe astonished and disabled at the same time in front of him.

And now 'Dorea' knows that he's on his way to Istanbul with India treasures. He followed him in a big fleet, hoping that he catch two birds with a single stone. But fastly, he dropped his dream when he realized what I sent 40 ships to support 'Salah Raiss'. He went away like he does, always seeking shelter in some Mediterranean harbors. After I conquered 27 islands and seven fortresses that were subject to Venice kingdom, I placed battalion over each one to protect and defend her.

I invaded 'Agribuse' and I imprisoned 20 000 individuals. I sent them all to Istanbul. I was informed that the greatest European fleets were assembled in this place. Thus, I sent 'Torgut Raiss' over twenty' kaderga' to discover the truth of the matter. But I couldn't be patient to await him. I went with a fleet from 'Agribuse' and I scanned the 'Mora' island coasts. When I reached 'Mudun', the crusaders gathered in 'Kurfu'. I started with 'Mudun' and I crossed the majority of 'Mora' south coasts, then to the north until I reached 'Arta' gulf.

The fortress of 'Brusa' was placed in north-west angle of this small gulf. His entrance was remarkably small. No ship can enter to it as it can be easily bombarded by the cannons of the Brusa castle. Carlos gathered the fleets of Malta, Florence, Albabawya (Catholic church) Genoa and Venice and placed her all under 'Andrea Doria' command. In my life, in history and even in books, I never heard about an immense fleet like that.

It was formed from more than 600 ships, including 306 military ones and 120 for soldiers carrying. And it's pushed by thousands of rowers.60 000 soldiers were brought in this fleet. Even some big ships transported 2000 soldiers once. It became like a heavy castle swimming in the sea. I had 122 'kaderga' ships, I haven't ships to soldiers transmission. In the open wars I didn't need a supporting ones.

For the fighters, I had 20 000 between sailors and cannons men.That way the entire number of soldiers between the two sides became 144 000.This assembly for the fight in the sea faces can't be seen or imagined by anyone.I invited the sea captains to the commandment ship and we discussed together. Despite the great courage of 'Torgut Raiss'and the sharp intelligence of 'Salah Raiss', they advised me to not leave the gulf until the crusaders leave it before us.

I didn't admit to this opinion, yes; I realized that the enemy is bigger than us in number three to four times, but our strength should be in an appropriate management of our fleet and protecting him from the destruction. Despite the significant difference in numbers and the situation that we had to face; we didn't another choice than we figure out how to win the battle. Fighting against an enormous fleet never heard or seen worldwide was a bad luck for me. But I wasn't able to leave our coasts open to the crusaders fleet. If I did this, how could I face my sultan tomorrow!

# Chapter 38: The Fight Of "Brusa"

I left the gulf after I took with me 'Torgut Raiss'. When Andrea Doria knew about that, he was shocked as he didn't expect I did this maneuver. He refused the fight at that day, he prefers preparing for the battle. When an issue opened for him in the northern west. He took his attention, waiting for the fight. In the next morning we find each other face to face like the last night.

I took my position over the Ottoman head fleet in the middle wing. They were with me my son ' Hasan Raiss' and my moral son 'Hasan Raiss' too. It was too over the middle wing of the fleet sheikh 'Ikhan Raiss', 'Jaafar Raiss' and 'Chaabane Raiss'. The right wing was under the command of 'Salah Raiss'. The left wing was under the command of the great savant and poet 'Syed Ali Raiss' (his best friend who wrote this autobiography dictated by Barbarossa). For ' Torgut Raiss', he was over the reserve fleet in behind.

And I placed the captains 'Sadek', 'Mehmet' and 'Gulze' under his orders. The enemy fleet was better than our in so many sides, but I have an advantage which is I command directly all my fleet wings. I was able to request fastly any ' kaderga' anywhere she would be. On the contrary, the enemy 'Dorea' could not do this. Even with the wings of his fleets, he wasn't able to command them. From other point too, the soldiers have different speaking languages, they can't cooperate closely.

The feelings of envy and hatred spread between them. As they were coming from different origins and countries. Much more the first venetian admiral 'Vincente Capellotoo' and the same 'Grimani Marco' for the Catholic fleet hate deeply 'Andrea Doria'. The other factor for our favor is the span of our cannons is much longer than theirs. Besides all this, we shouldn't forget that I put our ships in a special location helping us easily to destroy the enemy ones. Meanwhile, their shells fall away from us in the sea without touching us. This makes the kuffar captains stressed and angry without being able to do anything.

And suddenly, it coming an unexpected moment when 'Dorea' ordered his ships to approach our fleet. These orders were too late. It should be taken earlier. We could break their arrogance long time ago.With our speedy ships, we could surrounding their heavy ones until it was easy to put them in front of our cannons bombing them from any angle then retire speedily without being hurt. Our soldiers were too wearing light clothes and used light arms. Meanwhile, for the enemy, they wore heavy clothes covering their entire bodies and using heavy weapons, making their movements so difficult. Thus, our soldiers killed so many of them easily with the fewer losses on our side. Finally, our strong faith and our fellow to the world sultan were also factors in our win.

# Chapter 39: "Andrea Doria" Defeat

When the battle commenced, the south direction winds were against our ships. So I throw some papers written on it, some Quran verses. Then I made supplication for Allah to help and support us. In a short time, the winds calmed, then it reversed the direction in our favor! As I already said, 'Andrea Doria' finds himself imprisoned by the military maneuvers that I did. And based on her, he specifies the next step that he should do. He was in a worthless state when his fleet pieces dispersed under our shells bombing. I ordered 'Torgut Raiss' to pursue the kuffar ships.

When he found himself goes to the worser, 'Dorea' directed to shut the lights of his entire fleet than he instructed its retirement under the dark. This step reflects the insignificance of 'Dorea'. Besides, it was ominous on him and his fleet. This characterized by his escaping with the half of the fleet. But the majority of his ships touched by our shells, few of them saved. The half of the combined fleet between Spain, Venice and the Catholic Father, was settled on the sea ground. They were dreaming of taking the Mediterranean sea from us and seizing our kingdoms. Even, their stupid imagination makes them thinking to share the states of our sultan. And they agreed between them who own this state and the other one!

The battle extended for five hours, we lost through it some ships. After the pursuit in the dark, 'Torgut Raiss' could capture some touched ships by our shells. For me, I ordered my son 'Hasan Raiss' to travel to our sultan to notify him about our triumph. He reached him in 'Aderna' after 15 days of his leaving. The sultan at that time had come back from his campaign in 'Bugodan'.

He received him in his military camp in 'Yanbolo'. Our sultan directed to an assembly in his diwan (private council). When the diwan members were presents, 'Hasan Raiss' stand up and kissed the hands of his majesty. Then he read to him the triumph letter that I sent to him. The sultan thanks Allah for this accomplishment while he's standing up too. Before the sunset, he ordered festivities with this great doing.

I returned to Istanbul with the sultanate fleet. I found the happiness spread and shared between the citizens, expressing their content. After a rest for days, I left for 'Aderna' to meet the sultan, who received me in his private council. I spent days narrating to him all the incidents and events that we lived during this battle. The next year, I exited over the head fleet to 'Adriatic' sea. In this campaign, 'Torgut Raiss' and his son-in-law 'Hasan Raiss', could extract 'Nova' fortress from Venice kingdom. Thus, she requested peace accord that we did after she left for us several numbers of islands and castles and she paid us big refunds.

# Chapter 40: Shame On Carlos

After 'Brusa' battle, Carlos desperated from the collapse of Ottomans in the sea large. He decided to direct his concentration to control north Africa where my son 'Hasan Raiss' was its ruler as a representative for me, the' Beylar Bey. And when he seized Carlos' castle in Gibraltar strait with 30 'kaderga', the Spaniards became more desperate and Carlos' behaviors became inciting for the treason because he wanted to drop me in a trap. He invited me to betray my country, my religion, my sultan and my people.

He addressed me a letter stating: "*Your descent from the degree of the king to be just a 'Beylar Bey' as the Ottoman habits are a bad insult for you. That's why I suggest to you that you leave the sultan Suleiman service and I'll make you the ultimate king over all the African lands located between the red sea and the Atlantic ocean. At the same time, you should know that I don't request from you to be my ally, but it's sufficient to me that you stay my friend. And you cut your contacts with the Ottomans. That's all what I want from you*".

Immediately, I informed the sultanate council about Carlos letter. And I wrote a speech to the grand minister 'Lotfi Basha' before our going to Italy conquest telling him: "*Sir the Basha, I warn you from ignoring what Carlos prepares. When he'll realize that these tricks will not give results, he'll think of other satanic ones. I think he'll exploit my absence from Algiers and he will attack her".*

Lotfi Basha thought for a while, then he replied to me: *"Sir the Basha, You know the king Carlos more than me. You passed your life fighting him. Surely, you realize more than me the necessary care for Algiers, especially the fleet is under your orders. But my only advice for you that you don't react fastly to refuse the request of the king Carlos. You should try to waste his time as long as possible until the view be more clear".* Based on this dialog, I wrote to 'Andrea Doria' nominated by Carlos to negotiate with me, a neutral answer this is its content: *"I'm ready to negotiate with you concerning the offer of your king. But it can't be applied to Istanbul fearing that it arrives to the sultan. You should send a messenger to my son in Algiers Hasan Bey".* The trick worked and 'Dorea 'believed that I'm ready to betray my country. For me, I sent my secret instructions to my son Hasan about what he should do.

I ordered him too to distract Carlos messenger for a little of time. Throughout that, he should prepare the necessary waiting for the developing events. In a short period, the messengers of Carlos entered Algiers. The delegation was formed from 'Alonso Dealarcon', the captain 'Thergara' with a Jew physician from the ottoman empire inhabitants called 'Romeo'. After a while of negotiations, Hasan Bey, expelled the two Spanish messengers from Algiers. And he arrested the Jew physician as he was an Ottoman citizen.

He sent him to Istanbul, where I ordered his detention in 'Yedi Koleh'. The development of the events had imposing to us to not waste more time in distracting the king Carlos. But the mind of the Spaniards don't see like the Turkish mind does.

How is that? My son 'Hasan Bey' wrote to me that Carlos did with him the same thing like me. He messaged him and promised him to be the king of North Africa! And he instructed the Spanish governor on Wahran (Oran), 'Alkodet' to convince him about this treason.

I know 'Alkodet' as a fanatic infidel Spaniard, but at the same time, he was very courageous. He was aware that my son and my representative will never betray me or his country for a throne. I sent to him to continue distracting Alkodet. He wrote to him: "*You think that I can take the Algiers from the sultan Suleiman for what you suggest to me! No doubt that I want to take my place between the kings. But you should know when I advance a single step in this road, thousands of sailors camping over the Turkish fleet, will chain me and send me to Istanbul. For that, I see when your king will send his great fleets and anchoring on Algiers harbor, I will not defend the city. Thus, you can eliminate the Turkish fleet.When you'll seize the city, the entire Algeria will be for you*".

I was expecting with a little percentage that the conte 'Alkodet' and the Spanish king will swallow the bait easily. But their easy and speedy believe that me and my son Hasan accepts to betray our sultan, make my son himself stunned! Again, I wrote to Hasan to distract him until I came with the Ottoman fleet. But I shouldn't hurry as the other enemies fleets will not approach Algiers if they hear about an Ottoman fleet in the west of the Mediterranean. Like that, we spent three years after 'Brusa' battle and the Carlos political maneuvers. In the time when my sultan returning from his ninth campaign, Carlos was preparing his forces to invade Algiers.

It was clear that seizing of Algiers will threats the Ottoman existence in North Africa. The new fleet of Carlos was formed by 516 ships.274 ones were from 'kaderga' model. The rest were military ones for sea battles. This fleet was supported by 65 huge ships. Each one was like a castle swimming in the sea. The number of sailors except the rowers was 12330 and 23900 soldiers from the land forces. The total number of fighters is 36230 soldiers.. Besides all this, the crusades campaign was supported by different war battalions. There was no doubt that this campaign led by Carlos himself will finish by Algiers's occupation and seize. For that, the leaders of Europe and its nobles were wagering to participate in it beside their kings. It was on the front the famous nobles and princes of Spain, Germany and Italy.Whose insisted to accompany the king Carlos in this campaign.

# Chapter 41: King Carlos Message

Hasan Bey had 600 Turks and 2000 Arabic volunteers. To avoid the destruction of his fleet, it was necessary to move it away from Algiers' city. So it was natural that the majority of the sailors rode their ships and put her away from the harbor. In the day when Carlos was excited to invade Algiers; he wrote a letter to Hasan Bay telling him: "*The force that you see today, not just you but your grand master, can't push her. If you have two opened eyes and a mind, throw your weapon, tie your head with a hanky. And deliver me the keys of Algiers's castle. If you came to me and kiss the ground in front of me, I'll give you my amnesty. I'm the king of Spain, Sicily, Napoli, Netherlands, Belgium, America and the emperor of Germany. Your father and your master Barbarossa ran away from me in Tunis, fearing me. Be careful to not lose your mind and you put your sword in my face. Because if you'll do this, I swear with Jesus, I'll rip you and place your remains over Algiers tours*".

My son 'Kara Hasan Bey' answered him: "*The Algiers castle is not my property to deliver it to you. And I'll never give the land of my sultan Suleiman to lose the life and the afterlife. You should be aware that my heart has not any tiny fear of you.You spent your life receiving several disappointments from my father Khaireddine Basha. I'm confident that Allah will conquer me against you*". Carlos started attacking the castle, but the strong and courageous resistance that he saw made him stunned. When the evening came, he allowed his soldiers taking a rest. In the next morning, he was obliged to retire when he felt that his forces were nearly to be defeated.

The Algiers land was merged with the blood of my brother Arruj and so many of Turks coming from Ottoman areas. Does will stay for us or we will lose her? In a blessed night, the Spaniards descended hundreds of wine barrels from their ships and started drinking all the night, celebrating their expected occupation of Algiers city in the next morning. Meanwhile their celebration, the 600 Turks sailors sheltered in the castle haven't any feeling of fear the from infidel forces.. Hasan Bey infiltrated his spies between the enemy soldiers by wearing them the same uniforms.

So many of our soldiers were speaking Spanish as their native language. Between them, someones were prisoners for ten years rowing the Spaniards ships. The spies informed Hasan Basha of the enemy soldiers states. He realized that if he should do something, it must be this night. Otherwise, the matter will be worser in the morning.For that, he ordered his men, including the volunteers, to follow a mountain's way until they descend behind the Spanish camp. In the meantime, the moon cached behind the clouds, the deep dark is spreading. And the rain started falling strongly before being transformed to a storm.

Those signs made us feeling that Allah is with his mujahideen slaves supporting them. My men infiltrated in the enemy camps. The Spaniards were in majority losing consciousness beside this, the rain push them to solicit refuge under their tents. The guards left their stands and dispersed here and there. Each one of them search for a shelter from the storm. Oh Allah, you supported a few number of your servants against a huge army with this storm! The fleet of Carlos is floating hardly in this storm.

# Chapter 42: The Conqueror Turk

The help of Allah revealed in the fall of hailstones instead of rain. The size of every piece was the size of an egg. Enemy soldiers can't yet be protected under their tents. For the sea, it became boiling from the wind's power beside the hailstones like the water boiling over the fire. The kuffar tried to avoid the sinking of their ships and boats. In the midnight, Hasan Bey attacked their camp and put the sabers on their necks. The kuffar thought it was me. They screamed:" *Barbarossa returned from Istanbul. The grand Turk is coming*!"

Under the unexpected surprise, 3000 soldiers were once killed. The infidels didn't sleep until the morning. They received the sunrise in a miserable state. But the new day's surprise didn't leave them relaxing. The king Carlos was submerged with the feelings of angry and fear because he awaits for the apparition on the horizon for the ottoman sails at any moment. Despite the enemy situation, the situation of my son Hasan wasn't better. The Algiers inhabitants still remembering what occurred to Tunis and its people years ago from the Spaniards' massacres.

That's why they aimed that Turks surrendering. But the events show that who will stand up to the end, he will win. Carlos was in psychic turmoil as Allah apply on these infidels his angry. He ordered his soldiers to return to the fleet. And directed 'Andrea Doria' to move the ships away from Algiers. Hasan was watching the retirement of the enemy and the floods of soldiers arriving to the beach, pushing each other to ride the ships. Hasan took an advantage of this situation and make a sudden attack on them. when the bedouins saw the enemy retire, they would lose their minds from happiness. As a consequence, spontaneously, they went to the enemy soldiers, searching for the spoils.

The hungry and the thirst covered the Spaniards. They were exhausted. Even Carlos became unable to specify his next destination. His power vanished. Furthermore, he was ignoring the land that he wants to occupy. His war mistakes grew, and Hasan Bey exploited this to his favor. The enemy was obliged to descend his half fleet to the beach because of the hard storms. He couldn't attach the ships to avoid their retirement to the coast. Our soldiers could do this instead of the enemy and they could retire them to Algiers. Even they seized the cannons and all the military equipments.

With that way and in these circumstances, 20 000 infidels were ended between sinking or killed by the sailors' swords. The ones who survived were taken hostages. It was 4000 horses in the enemy fleet. Died, sank or slaughtered by the infidels whose later lost in the region and fell into the famine until they were obliged to eat their horses. These horses were from the most priceless beautiful ones. The Spaniards, who wore metallic dresses, were sinking in the mud lands. The cadavers were spread along the coasts and in the deep fields. When they ran away with their ships; they left many precious things to our sailors as they were preoccupied in escaping and surviving.

The Algiers city became more rich after this campaign. So many generals, admirals, captains, commanders, princes and princesses, nobles fell into detention. All of them were coming from the European capitals to enjoy seeing the occupation of Algiers. Even 'Andrea Doria' and others could save themselves with difficulty. This great tyrannical person burned thousands of people in the new world! He wanted to do the same with Algiers as he thought that it's like the new world. It's a serious tragedy for any Muslim city decline in his hands. How it will be her fate? He provided us an example years ago when he invaded Tunis city.

# Chapter 43: The King Horse

'Dorea' was bombarding the sailors with the shells which are in the majority couldn't touch them. Something pushed them to insist on revenging from him. In this campaign, the Christians used thousands of Muslims in rowing. Due to the storms, the majority of these victims sank into the sea. But the faith and the persistence of Hasan Bey helped him in the rescue of 1800 from them. For the admiral 'Dorea', his ship sank too. He was saved as he jumped from this ship to another one while sinking and he ran away. The situation of the crusaders was bad even the tongue is unable to describe it.

For the king Carlos, in the time when he governs half of Europe, he was defeated under the walls of Algiers. He was obliged to slay his stallion, as he didn't find anything to eat. When he was struggling to evade from the sea, he took his thrown from his head and throw it to the water expressing his extreme angry. He compared himself with our sultan Suleiman Khan despite his basic education wasn't military like our sultan and he has never led a military campaign on land by himself like our sultan. Over all this, he was ignorant about all the war laws and seas arts.

So how he considers defeating our sultan Suleiman Khan. This arrogant king was near to be a hostage but thanks to

'Malta Knights' (there's a state in UN today without people with this name and has embassies worldwide and this open big questions) and the few number of Hasan Bey men, he skipped. The crusaders fleet couldn't stay in the blessed Algiers land more than 13 days.

Meanwhile, three days were sufficient to delete him entirely. Then the conquered ships go to Spain full of crusaders fired by the Turks. This great defeat produced a huge echo in Europe. She made them unspeakable from the stunning. After this great triumph, my son Hasan became called 'The Conqueror'. His military grade was ' Bahia Sanjak Bey'. After this battle for a while, I visited its field. My delayed coming was because I wasn't predicting that the attack of Carlos on Algiers will be with this rapid manner.

The defeat of Carlos wasn't done by the hands of our sultan Suleiman Khan or his prime minister, the great chest, or even by one of his 'Beylar Beys' or me personally. It was by a captain of the sea. For a long time, Europe didn't live under a terrific defeat like this. That's why this one will be engraved in their history memory as will never recur again. This Carlos is the king who beat a famous king like the one of France called 'François le premier'. And he took him as a captive after a few hours duration of battle.

Later, my son Hasan extracted from the sinking ships 150 cannons which were maintained and retreated to Algiers.The number of hostages was very big, thus they were shared here and there like gifts. Because of this huge number, their prices dropped significantly in the slaves market. In other side, Hasan Bey charged 30 ships with the expensive, precious and valuable gifts to our sultan Suleiman Khan.

After my visit, I left to Istanbul that I reached after 21 days. The gifts offered to my sultan made other kings envy moving. The fleet of gifts was led by 'Delly Mehmet Raiss', who kissed my hands when he arrived in Istanbul. Where I discussed with him about his concerns and he delivered me the letter of my son Hasan Bey. I read this letter, and I was absolutely glad about its content. Then we go together to the sultan's palace, me in the front, then 'Mehmet Raiss 'then 30 captains. Accompanied by some sailors wearing clothes with golden lines and carrying the contributions that should be offered to our sultan.

# Chapter 44: The Sultanate Factory

The sultan Suleiman Khan just received me, 'Mehmet Raiss' and four or five from the highest ships commanders. The others were waiting outside his sultanate council. I delivered the letter sent by Hasan Bey. He opened her and read it by himself in the contrary to the habits in such cases. His face became shining, thus he ordered 200 dinars for the commanders and 100 dinars for each sailor.

He ordered too for the commanders a 'sultanate suit'. He generously accepted 1000 prisoners who will work as rowers. He gave my son too the grade of 'Beylar Bek' and 'Basha'. Surely Hasan will fly from happiness when he'll be aware of this honor from our sultan. He became in the same grade that I had earlier in Algiers. Some Algiers sailors were visiting Istanbul for the first time. Most of them were from Alanadhool small villages, traveled to Algiers and few of them coming from the big cities.

They were astonished of 'Bosphore' strait. They visited her castles, palaces and her secured walls. Their stunning was big, especially when they saw the ship's factory of our sultan with tens of thousands of workers there. Even near to 100 0000 worker! All of them working like the bees cells.

They thanked Allah as they belongs to a powerful country like this. I specified the sailors with different Turks sweets and food like the 'Baklawa' and other ones Meantime, they were received by palaces owners who love the guests and they treated them like 'Bashas', not as normal sailors. So many new youths come from Alanadhool seeking the sea jobs. I choose 300 who has some knowledge of the sea and I sent them to the captains. The rest I addressed them to the ships factory to be educated and working later there. Also, I equipped five 'kaderga' ships with all the necessary and directed 'Delly Mehmet' to deliver them to my son Hasan in Algiers. Later, he left Istanbul in 35 sea pieces.

My sultan exited to 'Saray Borno' to salute him. All the ships send shells to the air to goodbye and salute our sultan. After 17 days of travel, they reached Algiers. After a few days, our sultan sent other five ships to Hasan. He sent to him too a studded sword and a triumph 'Nishan' to put it on his turban head. A watch and a ring studded with diamonds. Besides the flags and the sultanate suit. With this honor, officially my son nominated 'Kara Hasan Basha'. Who later sent me 500 prisoners as a gift. I asked myself what should I do with all this number of slaves? Then I decided to offer them to the state. In other side, I was informed that Carlos spent entire months in a church never leaving it to another one. It was talk that he died from the oppression. And here I can put an end to my autobiography and thank Allah for giving me opportunities, the weak slave and servant, to serve my religion, my country and my glorious sultan.

# Don't miss out!

Visit the website below and you can sign up to receive emails whenever Mohamed Cherif publishes a new book. There's no charge and no obligation.

https://books2read.com/r/B-A-SXSU-XLNHD

**BOOKS 2 READ**

Connecting independent readers to independent writers.

Did you love *Pirate Red Beard Biography. The Complete Autobiography*? Then you should read *The Nazi UFOs Where Are They Now?*[1] by Mohamed Cherif!

2

-You must ask: Why it's called "Arctic Circle" before WW2 and then became "Antarctica" in the fifties ?

-The big question is if the Nazis' UFOs are real and exist really why they didn't overcome the USA in World War Two? Why they didn't attack and destroyed the USA and its allies France and the UK for Revenge after World War Two and until today?-What about the Nazis' UFOs Raid on Los Angeles killing Five American Citizens?-Then you should ask where are

1. https://books2read.com/u/3LV9O7

2. https://books2read.com/u/3LV9O7

they now, where they live. We live on six continents!-What are the different UFOs Nazis Programs?-The proof that the UFOs Nazis are still flying for 80 years Now.-What are the implications of Freemasonry in the Nazis' UFOs secret programs from the second world war until today?-What's about the continent after Antarctica never visited by a human as mentioned by The American Navy Admiral Richard Byrd on CBS television in 1955?-What about the strange voices or hums heard worldwide in the last twenty years, who is behind them?-What's about the sky Weaponization threat revealed by the Nasa Space program pioneer the Nazi Engineer Wernher Von Braun?-What about the manipulation of the physical properties of the ionosphere layer and its impact on climate and weather states?-What's the prepared scenario by Nazis and their colleagues in the USA and other countries?-The proofs in this book are clear and clean, you'll be surprised about the real face of the world that we live in and presented to us in a specific manner to stay hypnotized.

# Also by Mohamed Cherif

**Captain Barbarossa From A Pirate To An Admiral**
Captain Barbarossa: How I Became A Pirate?
Captain Barbarossa: Arruj Death
Captain Barbarossa : I Became An Admiral Over Ottoman
Empire Fleet


**Septembet 11th 2001 Attacks**
UA Flight 93.It Wasn't A Crash


**Standalone**
Mayas & Aliens
The Nazi UFOs Where Are They Now?
Islam As You Never Knew
Scientific Miracles Of Islam In Quran & Sunnah
La Vérité Sur Les Extraterrestres
Blue Beam Project A Zionists-Illuminatis Advanced Weapon
In the 21st Century
Truth About Extraterrestrials

Aliens & UFOs Then & Now
Pirate Red Beard Biography. The Complete Autobiography

# About the Author

Mohamed Cherif is a writer in different fields of knowledge, politics, and sciences. He has physics sciences master's degree. He writes in English and French languages. He has several books like Truth About Extraterrestrials, Hidden History of the Giants, Islam As You Never Knew, Blue Beam Project a Zionists-illuminatis Advanced Weapon for the 21 st Century. He is an environment Activist and supports Civil Societies and Anti-Tyranny movements around the world.